Also by Patrick Barry

Books

Good with Words: Speaking and Presenting

Good with Words: Writing and Editing

Notes on Nuance

Punctuation and Persuasion: Volume 1

The Syntax of Sports, Class 1: The Words under the Words

The Syntax of Sports, Class 2: The Power of the Particular

The Syntax of Sports, Class 3: The Rule of Three

The Syntax of Sports, Class 4: Parallel Structure

Online Courses

"Feedback Loops: How to Give and Receive High-Quality Feedback" (Coursera)

"Good with Words: Speaking and Presenting" (Coursera)

"Good with Words: Writing and Editing" (Coursera)

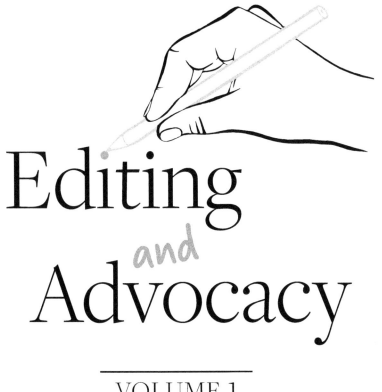

Editing
and
Advocacy

VOLUME 1

Patrick Barry

Feedback from students who have taken the class version of *Editing and Advocacy*:

"This is a class EVERYONE at the Law School should take."

"Professor Barry is a phenomenal professor who made me love writing."

"This course should be a requirement for graduation. Professor Barry prepares students to fulfill what the legal profession has been asking for a long time: excellent writers and attorneys that protect the integrity of the legal profession."

"Coming into law from a field where I did not have to do a lot of writing, I knew I was way behind my peers. Professor Barry has helped me close the gap. Out of all the classes I have taken, 'Editing and Advocacy' has been the most helpful."

"Professor Barry's teaching and materials have helped me immensely."

"Overall, I really enjoyed this class, and I really enjoyed Professor Barry. This will probably be the most useful class I take in law school."

"I learned a ton in this class."

"Professor Barry is one of the most wonderful instructors I have had the pleasure to encounter in my long university experience. My writing has improved immensely through his courses."

"Absolutely great class."

"Professor Barry not only did an excellent job of presenting the material. He also provided excellent advice for life."

"It is apparent that helping students learn to write and edit is truly what Professor Barry loves to do. His enthusiasm makes you want to learn the material and submit your best work. I tell everyone to take this class!"

"Patrick Barry is likely the best professor on campus."

"Professor Barry is one of the most clear and energetic professors I have had in law school. He incorporates teaching practical skills with general career and life lessons."

"Professor Barry is a truly talented teacher and has been wonderful to learn from."

Published in the United States of America by
Michigan Publishing
Manufactured in the United States of America

DOI: https://doi.org/10.3998/mpub.12540095

ISBN 978-1-60785-775-4 (paper)
ISBN 978-1-60785-776-1 (e-book)
ISBN 978-1-60785-777-8 (open-access)

An imprint of Michigan Publishing, Maize Books serves the publishing needs of the University of Michigan community by making high-quality scholarship widely available in print and online. It represents a new model for authors seeking to share their work within and beyond the academy, offering streamlined selection, production, and distribution processes. Maize Books is intended as a complement to more formal modes of publication in a wide range of disciplinary areas. http://www.maizebooks.org

For James Boyd White.
This book is better because I have read so many of his.

Poetry is everywhere; it just needs editing.

—James Tate, winner of the 1992 Pulitzer Prize in Poetry

CONTENTS

CONTENTS

INTRODUCTION

I like to replace a humdrum word with one that has more precision or color. I like to strengthen the transition between one sentence and another. I like to rephrase a drab sentence to give it a more pleasing rhythm or a more graceful musical line. With every small refinement I feel that I'm coming nearer to where I would like to arrive, and when I finally get there I know it was the rewriting, not the writing, that won the game.

—William Zinsser, *On Writing Well* (1976)

What is the optimal amount of advocacy?

My law students and I face that question all the time. We face it when we're drafting motions. We face it when we're proposing changes to contracts. We even face it when putting together key emails, text messages, and social media posts.

In all these situations and many more, we don't want to oversell our arguments and ideas—but we don't want to undersell them either. Instead, we hope to hit that perfect sweet spot known as "persuasion."

We don't always succeed, but one thing that has significantly increased our effectiveness is the amount of time we spend on an important skill: editing.

A. Editing vs. Proofreading

When I say "editing," I don't mean "proofreading." Many people think editing and proofreading are identical skills. They're not. Proofreading involves catching typos and fixing formatting. It cultivates a host of admirable qualities—patience, thoroughness, attention to detail—but it doesn't require a whole lot of imagination.

Editing, on the other hand, is a fundamentally creative act. Good editors don't just see the sentence that was written. They see the sentence that *might* have been written. They know how to spot words that shouldn't be included and summon up ones that haven't yet appeared. Their value comes not just from preventing mistakes but also from discovering new ways to improve a piece's style, structure, and overall impact.

It's important to learn how to add this kind of value. Whatever your cause or client base, poor editing skills can painfully limit the help you're able to provide, not to mention the heights to which you can take your own career. It is tough to produce quality work if you don't know your way around a sentence.

And given how collaborative many organizations and movements have become, you're certainly going to want to know your way around other people's sentences too. Advocates who improve the projects they are asked to review are extremely valuable commodities.

Imagine, for example, that you heard someone described in the following way: "Whenever I give them a draft, it always comes back better."

Wouldn't you want to work with that person? Wouldn't you want to give them your drafts as well?

Of all the reasons someone might get passed over for a project or promotion, I doubt any has ever been, "We can't work with them. Their edits are too good."

B. Vehicles (and Long Sentences) in the Park

To test your own editing skills, consider the sentence below. It was written by a law student whose assignment may bring back memories—if you're a lawyer—of when you first learned how to interpret statutes, particularly if your professor was a fan of the legal philosopher H. L. A. Hart. The student was asked to decide whether a park's ban on "vehicles" extends to bicycles. (Hart first posed this "Vehicles in the Park" hypothetical in the *Harvard Law Review* back in 1958.) Here's a sample of what the student wrote:

> Given the fact that the statute allows the presence of bicycles so long as they are being more well controlled by pushing them rather than riding them, it seems the intent of the rule is not that no vehicles at all should be allowed but that the environment of the park should be one where there are no fast-moving vehicles in areas where pedestrians may be enjoying a leisurely stroll.

Suppose the student asked you for some feedback on this sentence. What changes would you recommend?

I'll offer my own suggestions in a moment. But first I want to flag that better proofreading won't be enough to fix the sentence's many problems. The sentence doesn't contain any misspelled words. Nor does it have any grammatical gaffes. And the only bits of punctuation (the comma after "them" and the period after "stroll") don't raise major red flags. If we really want to improve the sentence—if we want to turn it into something we'd feel comfortable putting in front of a judge or client—we'll need to move beyond proofreading and instead do some serious editing.

C. The Virtue of Clarity

A good place to start would be to urge the student to become better friends with the most underused punctuation mark in formal writing, especially among highly educated people: the period. Inserting a period in the right place will transform the student's seventy-word behemoth of a sentence into a much more digestible set of two sentences.

Making this edit would also helpfully push the student toward "the virtue of clarity," a term I borrow from an observation the Australian writer Clive James once made about his literary hero, the American critic and novelist Edmund Wilson. According to James, Wilson achieved the virtue of clarity by doing something as simple as it is rare. When writing, he tried to just say one thing at a time.*

Lawyers often have the opposite tendency. We try to say everything at once. That's fine for a first draft or even a second, third, or fourth draft. At those stages, we're still figuring out the connections among our ideas and arguments. Letting our minds roam a bit can be creatively useful. A run-on sentence or two might very well lead to a

---

* In Chapter 3 of an earlier book, *Good with Words: Speaking and Presenting*, we learned about how "the virtue of clarity" can also be helpful to keep in mind when communicating out loud. (It's a pretty versatile virtue.)

helpful discovery, as proponents of "freewriting," such as Peter Elbow of the University of Massachusetts–Amherst, often attest.

But the calculation switches when it's time for the final draft, the draft you plan to send out into the world and impose on your target audience's brain. With that draft, it's important to slow down, revise carefully, and deliver your thoughts in a package that is easy for people to process. Had the "Vehicles in the Park" student done that, we might have seen the following transformation:

> **Original Version:** "Given the fact that the statute allows the presence of bicycles so long as they are being more well controlled by pushing them rather than riding them, it seems the intent of the rule is not that no vehicles at all should be allowed but that the environment of the park should be one where there are no fast-moving vehicles in areas where pedestrians may be enjoying a leisurely stroll." (1 sentence: 70 words.)

> **Edited Version:** "The rule's intent is not to ban all vehicles, because bikes are allowed if pushed. The rule's intent is to ensure a park environment free of fast-moving vehicles." (2 sentences: 28 words.)

D. Changeable

Plenty of other ways to revise the student's sentence exist. When it comes to editing, there is rarely a single right answer. You can take a particular set of words in a seemingly infinite number of directions.

Which is why I said editing is a fundamentally creative act. Editors add. Editors delete. Editors separate, combine, and rearrange. The best ones never consider a piece of writing to be unimprovable.

Instead, they embrace what the literary critic M. H. Abrams once identified as the hardest part about learning to write: realizing that what you put down on paper is "changeable." "Students tend to freeze at the first effort," Abrams explained in a 2007 interview. "The breakthrough comes when they realize that they can make it better—can identify what their purposes were and realize better ways to achieve those purposes. That is the important thing in teaching students to write: not to be frozen in their first effort."

This book is designed to showcase that inventive flexibility. We'll cover the mechanics of editing. We'll cover the psychology of editing. We'll also cover how to even find *time* for editing, especially because "underbusy" is probably not an adjective many of us would use to describe our current lives.

First, though, I want to share a little bit about my teaching style and how that might affect your reading experience. The next section covers both of those topics.

TEACHING STYLE AND READING TIPS

My approach to teaching focuses on three things:

1. Creating an engaging conceptual *vocabulary* people can use and share.
2. Providing plenty of opportunities for *low-stakes practice*.
3. Helping people apply what they've learned to *high-stakes projects*.

With these goals in mind, I want to offer a few tips on how you can get the most out of this book.

Vocabulary

Each chapter begins with some conceptual vocabulary designed to provide you with a better sense of the mechanics and strategy of effective editing. Some of the terms may be familiar to you. Others may  not. The best way to increase your fluency with the whole set is to start using the terms yourself. What the science journalist Brooke Jarvis has pointed out about wine experts—that they learn to identify the distinct aromas of merlots and Chardonnays by "learning a language for them"—is also, I think, true of editing experts. Without labels for things, it can be hard to move beyond a superficial understanding of a subject or skill, let alone make meaningful progress toward mastery.

So as you move through this book, consider periodically taking a break to summarize a chapter—or even just a couple of paragraphs—to a friend or family member. Your first attempts may be a bit awkward and incomplete. Mine usually are.

But the process of regularly retrieving, processing, and then articulating your newly acquired knowledge will, a lot of research shows, have lasting benefits. Education works better when it is coproduced.

Low-Stakes Practice

You can't become a better editor if you don't actually edit. Nobody improves the way they revise sentences just by looking at them.

For this reason, there will be many low-stakes opportunities to practice the techniques we'll be learning. To help with that, I recommend keeping a notebook nearby as you make your way through the material. You can use a physical notebook. You can use a digital notebook. You can use any kind of notebook you want. Even just writing on a piece of scrap paper could work.

The point is to create a space for yourself that is free of judgment, consequence, or anything else that may make you anxious about putting words down on a page. Without low-stakes practice, it is tough to achieve long-term growth.*

High-Stakes Projects

As helpful as low-stakes practice can be, I also encourage you to use this book to pursue at least one high-stakes project. Summarizing decades of research and hundreds of studies, the psychologists Edwin Locke and Gary Latham have concluded that "high, or hard, goals are motivating because they require one to attain more in order to be satisfied." These types of goals "lead to greater effort and/or persistence than do moderately difficult, easy, or vague goals."

Maybe your high-stakes project will involve editing something you've written for work or school. Or maybe you'll focus on something more personal, like a love letter, a thank-you note, or a difficult

---

* If you want additional opportunities for low-stakes practice, check out the online series "Good with Words: Writing and Editing" (https://www.coursera .org/specializations/good-with-words) on the educational platforms Coursera or FutureLearn. People who have already completed that series will notice that this book tries to capture, in written form, a lot of the material included there.

email you've been meaning to send. The important thing isn't the form or the subject matter. The important thing is the value you place on the outcome. We use low-stakes practice to prepare us for high-stakes situations.

PART I

For the prose writer: success consists in felicity of verbal expression, which every so often may result from a quick flash of inspiration but as a rule involves a patient search for the "mot juste," for the sentence in which every word is unalterable, the most effective marriage of sounds and concepts . . . concise, concentrated, and memorable.

—Italo Calvino, *Six Memos for the Next Millennium* (1988)

CHAPTER 1

Editing and Empathy

*All advocacy is, at its core, an
exercise in empathy.*

—Former US ambassador to the United Nations
Samantha Power, "Commencement Address
at the University of Pennsylvania" (2015)

"Design begins with empathy." I once wrote those words on the chalkboard during a class for students in the Child Welfare Appellate Clinic at the University of Michigan Law School. I thought it might help them with the legal briefs they were about to write, many of which would take up the cause of a mother or father who recently had their parental rights unconstitutionally terminated.*

I borrowed the words from Ilse Crawford, whose work as an interior designer can be seen all over the world—from airport lounges in Hong Kong, to fancy restaurants in London, to pear-shaped stools at IKEA. In Crawford's view, "empathy is a cornerstone of design."

She thinks it's important to understand the spaces and products she creates from the perspective of the people who use them. How easily can a busy waiter pick up a chair and move it to the other side of the table? How quickly can a jet-lagged traveler settle into a daybed and start to relax? What do people actually use a ceramic pitcher to pour?

The students in the class had been told over and over again that "Who is the audience?" is the first question to ask when approaching any piece of writing—be it a brief, an email, or even a postcard. But introducing the term "empathy" into the conversation seemed to help them think more critically and concretely about what that question really means. So did asking them to imagine what a full day might look like in the life of the Court of Appeals judges to whom they'd soon be submitting their briefs. How packed is each judge's schedule? How big is their to-do list? What things, people, and remembered

---

* Thanks to the excellent work of Tim Pinto and Vivek Sankaran, the two law professors who run the clinic, the students' briefs have been remarkably effective over the years. Appeals to overturn these kinds of parental terminations are typically successful 2–5 percent of the time. Appeals written by the students, however, have been successful over 50 percent of the time. That's a lot of reunited families.

priorities are going to interrupt them as they try to read through the piles of documents on their desks?

Too often advocates of all kinds skip over these types of considerations. We rush to cram as much information as possible into our arguments and explanations, forgetting that an overstuffed brief, memo, or report is not at all user-friendly. Judges and other key decision-makers already have many other overstuffed things in their lives: calendars, briefcases, court dockets, email inboxes. Why tax their brains (and their time) even more? Why not instead begin by thinking about what kind of document you would like to read if you were in their position? Why not start with empathy?

A. Strategic Empathy

You might even think of this use of empathy in strategic terms. It's goal-oriented compassion. The more accurately you imagine what it's like to be the people you are trying to persuade, the more likely you'll be to craft a message that successfully addresses their particular concerns and preferences. That's one of the reasons why, in the legal world, a judge's former law clerks are such coveted sources of information. They've worked with the judge and been involved in past decisions. They know the pet peeves to avoid and the key issues to highlight. They, in short, have inside intel. It's tough to imagine a more valuable focus group.

But even if your industry or field doesn't have the equivalent of former law clerks, it can still be useful to take a moment to think about, in detail, the reading experience of the people you're attempting to target. Advocacy, in a wide variety of arenas, requires empathizing with your clients and convincing important gatekeepers to do the same. But extending that empathetic function to the gatekeepers themselves might be beneficial as well.

Maybe a more empathetic version of ourselves would write shorter documents. Maybe we'd write more vivid documents. Maybe we'd identify our main point more clearly and inspect our sentences more scrupulously, realizing that busy readers have little time—and even less patience—for irrelevant information and unprofessional punctuation.

Maybe we'd even approach revisions a bit like the fiction writer George Saunders does.

B. George Saunders

"For people who pay close attention to the state of American fiction, George Saunders has become a kind of superhero," gushed an in-depth profile of Saunders in the *New York Times* in 2013. "His stories now appear regularly in the *New Yorker*, he has been anthologized all over the place, and he has won a bunch of awards, among them a 'genius grant' in 2006 from the MacArthur Foundation, which described him as a 'highly imaginative author [who] continues to influence a generation of young writers and brings to contemporary American fiction a sense of humor, pathos and literary style all his own."

Ever since that profile appeared, Saunders's reputation has only grown, thanks in part to *Lincoln in the Bardo*, a novel that earned him the 2017 Man Booker Prize for the creative way it explores the grief Abraham Lincoln must have felt when his eleven-year-old son, Willie, died halfway through Lincoln's first presidential term. In that novel and in all the other books Saunders has published, he tries to have empathy not just for his characters but also for his readers. In his

view, revision is ultimately about imagining your readers to be "as humane, bright, witty, experienced, and well-intentioned as you." You need to find a way, he says, to "welcome [them] in."

Some of the qualities that Saunders ascribes to his ideal readers might seem tough to square with the everyday realities of being an advocate, especially if your past encounters with a particular judge, adversary, or official have been at best unencouraging and at worst downright nasty. Trying to empathize with a blowhard can be a waste of time.

Yet the generosity that motivates Saunders's method may nevertheless be worth adopting. The best pieces of persuasive writing are cognitive gifts to people who depend on them to make important decisions. They highlight the relevant facts. They address the salient objections. And they proceed with a rhythm and honesty that communicate a powerful combination of trust and expertise.

They essentially say to the decision-makers, "Look, I know you have a really difficult job to do. So read me. I can help."

C. RBG

The upcoming Low-Stakes Practice section in this chapter focuses on someone who was an expert in this kind of writing: Justice Ruth Bader Ginsburg of the US Supreme Court. Long before being nominated to sit on the court, Ginsburg represented clients herself. The briefs she submitted were so well reasoned, well structured, and well edited that they were essentially "a judicial opinion on a silver platter," according to the renowned constitutional law scholar Geoffrey Stone.

Stone made this observation during a public conversation he had with Ginsburg at the University of Chicago Law School in 2013. "That was always my aim," Ginsburg explained. "When I wrote briefs, I wanted to give the Court something that the Court could convert into an opinion."

She more than succeeded. In several landmark cases—including *Frontiero v. Richardson*, *Reed v. Reed*, and *Craig v. Boren*—Ginsburg was able to get the court to rethink its earlier positions on gender discrimination and secure important, paradigm-shifting protections for women under the Fourteenth Amendment. She understood the obstacles that the justices faced. She gave them the operative details and conceptual tools they needed to rule in her favor. And she did it all with a kind of understated charm and forthrightness that led her to become, in the words of her good friend (and ideological opposite) Justice Antonin Scalia, "the Thurgood Marshall of [women's rights]." That's strategic empathy at its best.

Low-Stakes Practice: Adapting Ideas
to People and People to Ideas

It is true, is it not, that in the argument of an appeal the advocate is angling, consciously and deliberately angling, for the judicial mind. Whatever tends to attract judicial favor to the advocate's claim is useful. Whatever repels it is useless or worse. The whole art of the advocate consists in choosing the one and avoiding the other.
—John W. Davis, "The Argument of an Appeal" (1940)

This Low-Stakes Practice exercise reinforces the idea that good advocates edit with empathy. They always think about how to adapt, in the words of the rhetorician Donald Bryant, "ideas to people and people to ideas."

You'll begin by reading a passage from *Ruth Bader Ginsburg: A Life* by the award-winning historian Jane S. de Hart. The passage describes Justice Ginsburg's legal strategy in *Moritz v. Commissioner of Internal Revenue*, the first gender-discrimination case she helped out with, over twenty years before she became a Supreme Court justice.

As you move through the passage, you may notice something odd: it isn't particularly well written. That's because I've added a lot of unnecessary words to de Hart's sentences. To some sentences, I've added unnecessary words at the beginning. To others, I've added them to the middle and end. My hope is to make the time you spend navigating the whole set feel like a bit of a chore.

I've created this difficulty because I want to give you a chance to practice editing with the reader's experience in mind. Ginsburg was someone who, as the passage makes clear, thought carefully about the effect her words had on her audience. She knew that alienating people isn't a smart way to try to persuade them, particularly if those people are wearing black robes and holding a gavel.

She also knew—thanks to a literature course she took in college with the legendary novelist Vladimir Nabokov—the power  that comes with being able to tell a vivid, compelling story. Here's how Ginsburg, in an essay published in the *New York Times* in 2016, explained the course's long-term influence on her: "Words could paint pictures, I learned from [Nabokov]. Choosing the right word, and the right word order, he illustrated, could make an enormous difference in conveying an image or an idea."

In an interview around the same time, she mentioned a second professor who played a big role in shaping her writing style: the constitutional law scholar Robert Cushman. "In his gentle way," Ginsburg said of Cushman, for whom she worked as a research assistant, "he suggested that my writing was a bit elaborate. I learned to cut out unnecessary adjectives and to make my compositions as spare as I could."

Try to take a similar approach when editing the doctored passage below. Focus on spotting and removing the excess words I injected. Then check the answer key to get a sense of how the passage actually appears in de Hart's book. You might not agree with every choice she made. But you'll at least get to compare your version to hers. Testing your editorial intuitions against the final draft of an accomplished author can be instructive, even illuminating.

Doctored Passage: "The case would certainly have to be made extremely narrowly with no overreaching and overdone claims for gender justice and fairness. Instead, she was determined to paint the plaintiff's plight so extremely vividly that from even the briefest description Charles Moritz's voice would emerge as a genuine real person—a skill harking back to Nabokov's word pictures, which she would make sure to continue to hone in all of her future cases. The legal arguments on Moritz's behalf would be fully supported with case citations in the brief. And never, never, she vowed, would she be threatening or emotional or hysterical. Instead rather, she must lead the judges to the desired judgment in a way that was perfectly comfortable to them. Moritz very much deserved to win. But her larger and more important goal remained that of establishing equal protection as a completely viable weapon with which to attack sex discrimination in every aspect of the law."

Note: If it helps to know, the original passage by de Hart contains 128 words. My intentionally bloated version contains 157 words. That gives you 29 words to target. If you find more than that, great. Perhaps you can make the sentences even more user-friendly than de Hart did.

Answer Key

The unnecessary words I added are underlined:

> The case would <u>certainly</u> have to be made <u>extremely</u> narrowly with no overreaching <u>and overdone</u> claims for gender justice <u>and fairness</u>. Instead, she <u>was</u> determined to paint the plaintiff's plight so <u>extremely</u> vividly that from even the briefest description Charles Moritz's voice would emerge as a <u>genuine</u> real person—a skill harking back to Nabokov's word pictures, which she would <u>make sure to</u> continue to hone in <u>all of her</u> future cases. <u>The</u> legal arguments on Moritz's behalf would be fully supported with case citations in the brief. And never, never, she vowed, would she be threatening or emotional <u>or hysterical</u>. <u>Instead</u> rather, she must lead the judges to the desired judgment in a way that was <u>perfectly</u> comfortable to them. Moritz <u>very much</u> deserved to win. But her larger <u>and more important</u> goal remained that of establishing equal protection as a <u>completely</u> viable weapon with which to attack sex discrimination in <u>every aspect of</u> the law.

Here's the leaner version that actually appeared in de Hart's book.

> The case would have to be made narrowly with no overreaching claims for gender justice. Instead, she determined to paint the plaintiff's plight so vividly that from even the briefest description Charles Moritz's voice would emerge as a real person—a skill harking back to Nabokov's word pictures, which she would continue to hone in future cases. Legal arguments on Moritz's behalf

would be fully supported with case citations in the brief. And never, never, she vowed, would she be threatening or emotional. Rather, she must lead the judges to the desired judgment in a way that was comfortable to them. Moritz deserved to win. But her larger goal remained that of establishing equal protection as a viable weapon with which to attack sex discrimination in the law.

High-Stakes Project: Teachers vs. Readers

Here, the many degrees I spent years accumulating amounted to naught. The [editors] had discovered within days that, beneath the complex sentences and high-falutin language, I really had no idea how to write for a general audience.

—Bo Seo, *Good Arguments* (2022)

Background

In a widely viewed YouTube lecture called "The Craft of Writing Effectively," Larry McEnerney of the University of Chicago candidly addresses an important fact: a lot of us have spent many years in an educational system in which people—namely, our teachers—were paid to read our writing and care about the ideas we communicate.

If you're still in school, it's worth considering what is going to happen when you graduate and enter a world in which that kind of subsidized attention is no longer available. How might your current approach to writing need to change once it is no longer a given that anyone will be interested in what you have to say?

If you're not in school, what has the transition to not having a captive audience been like? What adjustments have you made to the way you present your thoughts, knowing full well that many emails, reports, memos, and other things you write will, at best, get skimmed and, at worst, be completely ignored?

As the technology columnist Farhad Manjoo explains in a piece aptly titled "You Won't Finish This Article," the abundance of immediately available media options—from Netflix to podcasts to Twitter—means that "it's easier than ever, now, to switch to something else." Manjoo then shares that in the past year "my wife and I have watched at least a half-dozen movies to about the 60 percent mark" and that "there are several books on my Kindle I've never experienced past Chapter 2."

"Maybe this is just our cultural lot," he continues. "We live in the age of skimming. I want to finish the whole thing, I really do. I wish you would, too. . . . But who am I kidding. I'm busy. You're busy. There's always something else to read, watch, play, or eat."

Assignment

As you begin to work on your high-stakes project, keep the insights of both McEnerney and Manjoo in mind. Focus on your particular audience. Who are they? What do they care about? Why should they be interested in what you have to say?

Even if they are interested, you still need to think hard—though also with compassion and understanding—about the many other things that will be competing for their attention. Do they have kids? Do they get a lot of emails and requests? Is a small slot late at night, early in the morning, or during their commute the only space in their schedule for any kind of reading, let alone the extra bit you're now asking them to add to their already full plate?

In many ways, these questions are similar to the ones we asked earlier in the chapter, when we were trying to imagine the daily demands on the judges my law students were trying to persuade. Failing to realize that pretty much all readers are busy readers is a big mistake.

* * *

To demonstrate how the "strategic empathy" mentioned in the Vocabulary part of the chapter can be applied to a wide range of high-stakes projects and audiences, here are a couple of possibilities. Each example is based on ones chosen by various students of mine.

> **High-Stakes Project:** Publish an Op-Ed
> **Audience:** The newspaper's or website's editors
> **Questions:**
> - How old are the editors of the publication you are targeting?

- What is their likely political outlook, socioeconomic status, and educational background?
- Which topics and viewpoints will they find fresh, relevant, and valuable?
- Which will they find stale, trivial, and a waste of journalistic space?
- How many submissions do you think these editors have to review each week?
- How often do they get interrupted each day?
- On what device will they be reading what you wrote—a laptop, a desktop, their phone?
- What kind of Op-Ed (and author) will their boss be glad they decided to publish?

High-Stakes Project: Get a job
Audience: Hiring committee
Questions:

- How many applications will there be for this position?
- How long will the committee members spend looking at each candidate?
- What are some things they'll likely find to be unhelpful, even annoying, in applications?
- What are some things they'll likely find to be interesting and useful?
- Besides reviewing applications, what does the typical day of these committee members consist of? How many meetings? How many phone calls? What deadlines and obligations will be on their mind when they finally get to your materials?

CHAPTER 2

Editing and Interleaving

*When you space out practice at a task
and get a little rusty between sessions,
or you interleave the practice of two or
more subjects, retrieval is harder and feels
less productive, but the effort produces
longer lasting learning and enables more
versatile application of it in later settings.*

—Peter Brown, Henry Roediger, and Mark McDaniel,
Make It Stick: The Science of Successful Learning (2014)

A learning technique called "interleaving"—which involves strategically switching between different topics or forms of practice—has helpfully started to make its way into the study tips that college and law students receive. Journal articles promote interleaving. Popular websites promote interleaving. And so do a wider variety of university research centers devoted to improving educational outcomes.

This chapter, however, suggests that interleaving has an additional application, one that can help not just students but also journalists, judges, consultants, scientists, bloggers, and anybody else whose professional success depends on efficiently managing multiple writing projects. Just as interleaving can make study sessions more productive, it can also make editing sessions more productive.

A. Learning and Forgetting

The leading proponent of "interleaving" is the psychologist Robert Bjork, who runs the Learning and Forgetting Lab at UCLA. "Particularly when one has several different things to learn," explains his lab's website, "an effective strategy is to interleave one's study: Study a little bit of history, then a little bit of psychology followed by a chapter of statistics and go back again to history. Repeat."

A key aspect of this approach is a concept Bjork calls "desirable difficulties." There is something helpfully hard about following up a study session on, say, constitutional law with a study session on contracts instead of just doubling up on constitutional law. The cognitive work it takes to switch subjects has been shown to produce much deeper and longer-lasting comprehension. You can think of it as a form of intellectual cross-training. Your mental muscles become stronger and more flexible when they are regularly stretched in different ways.

A related technique is "spacing." It involves strategically planning out your study sessions so that there are significant breaks between them. That way, your brain can put in a useful amount of effort to remember what you previously covered, a process that establishes more powerful—and more permanent—neural pathways to the information. Here's how Bjork explains the payoff: "When we access things from our memory, we do more than reveal it's there. It's not like a playback. What we retrieve becomes more retrievable in the future. Provided the retrieval succeeds, the more difficult and involved the retrieval, the more beneficial it is."

For this reason, students of all kinds should spend *less* time simply rereading their notes or highlighting material and *more* time quizzing themselves. Tools like flash cards push you beyond just recognizing material and move you toward the more useful task of retrieving it.

You might even consider reducing the amount of notes you take in class or in a meeting. Instead, wait to memorialize your thoughts until after the class or meeting ends. Recalling content you've been taught is more effective than thoughtlessly copying down everything the teacher or presenter says.

B. The Poet Is Working

The more I learned about interleaving and spacing, the more I began to wonder whether these techniques might be usefully applied to writing and editing. If there are cognitive benefits and productivity gains to switching between study subjects, might there also be cognitive benefits and productivity gains to switching between writing projects?

A visit to one of my classes by Jeffrey Fisher, the codirector of the Supreme Court Litigation Clinic at Stanford Law School and one of the most accomplished appellate lawyers in the country, encouraged me to pursue that hunch. He told the students that he regularly works on three briefs at once. Going back and forth between cases, he said, helps him spot and correct the errors in each brief.

An article in the *Chronicle of Higher Education* called "The Habits of Highly Productive Writers" supports Fisher's approach. Along with observations that highly productive writers "leave off at a point where it will be easy to start again" and "don't overtalk their projects," the author of the piece, Rachel Toor, suggests that highly productive writers also work on multiple projects at once. "Some pieces need time to smolder," she explains. "Leaving them to turn to something short and manageable makes it easier to go back to the big thing. Fallowing and crop rotation lead to a greater harvest."

Another benefit of interleaving is nicely articulated by something Toor notes later in her piece: a lot of writing gets done when you're not actually writing. She quotes a passage from the novel *The End of the Affair* by Graham Greene to illustrate what she means:

> So much in writing depends on the superficiality of one's days. One may be preoccupied with shopping and income tax returns and chance conversations, but the stream of the unconscious continues to flow, undisturbed, solving problems, planning ahead: one sits down sterile and dispirited at the desk, and suddenly the words come as though from the air: the situations that seemed blocked in a hopeless impasse move forward: the work has been done while one slept or shopped or talked with friends.

Perhaps an easier, more playful way to remember this idea is through an anecdote that the French writer André Breton tells about a fellow poet. The poet apparently used to hang a notice on the door of his house every evening before he went to sleep. The notice stated, "THE POET IS WORKING."

The implication of the notice: My brain is creating even when the rest of me is asleep. Or as John Steinbeck, who won the 1962 Nobel Prize in Literature for such American classics as *The Grapes of Wrath* and *Of Mice and Men*, once remarked, "It is a common experience that a problem difficult at night is resolved in the morning after the committee of sleep has worked on it."

C. Blocking vs. Interleaving

An important qualification about interleaving needs to be made. If you don't start projects, the parts of your brain that could help you out while you are sleeping or are off doing something else will not have any material with which to work. Those parts will also have less overall time to come up with ideas and solutions.

Consider Jeffrey Fisher again, the superstar Supreme Court advocate. Suppose he has three briefs to write in the same thirty-day month. He could focus entirely on the first brief during the initial ten days, entirely on the second brief during the second ten days, and entirely on the third brief during the last ten days.

But that strategy—which education experts call "blocking"— would limit, to just ten days, the amount of time Fisher gives his subconscious to help with each brief. By instead interleaving and periodically switching among the three briefs over the course of the whole month, he increases the help he gets. His subconscious now has closer to the full thirty days to tinker, strategize, reverse course, rearrange arguments, generate new ideas, and do all the other mental work that good editing requires. He also enjoys the added bonus of not getting so wrapped up in one brief that he loses the ability to step back and revise it with a sharp editorial eye.

The psychologist Adam Grant highlights a related set of benefits in "Why I Taught Myself to Procrastinate," an essay he published in the *New York Times* in 2016. The youngest professor to earn tenure at the Wharton Business School, Grant is the kind of person who, in college, completed his senior thesis four weeks before it was due and, in graduate school, submitted his dissertation two years in advance. "For years," he explains in the essay, "I believed that anything worth doing was worth doing early."

His perspective changed, however, when he began collaborating with Jihae Shin, who now teaches at the University of Wisconsin School of Business. Through a combination of experiments and survey data, Shin assembled a range of evidence showing that procrastination can actually lead to a boost in creative thinking—at least when done in a certain way. You don't get the boost if your procrastination prevents you from starting a task in the first place. You only get it if you do your procrastinating sometime between when you start and when you finish.

"Our first ideas, after all, are usually our most conventional," explains Grant, who eventually teamed up with Shin to publish a related set of findings. "My senior thesis in college ended up replicating a bunch of existing ideas instead of introducing new ones. When you procrastinate, you're more likely to let your mind wander. That gives you a better chance of stumbling onto the unusual and spotting unexpected patterns."

Grant then shares how Shin's research prompted him to tinker with his previously hyperfocused approach to writing and editing. Instead of single-mindedly pursuing one project until it was completely finished, he intentionally put the project aside once he got through a first draft. After returning to the draft three weeks later, the payoff was clear. "When I came back to it, I had enough distance to wonder, 'What kind of idiot wrote this garbage?' To my surprise, I had some fresh material at my disposal."

Three weeks may seem like a long time to leave a document dormant, especially if court deadlines or client delivery dates are soon approaching. But even taking a few days—or simply a couple of hours—can help. The point is to free up the mental space needed to view your writing through a more creative and discerning compositional lens.

Plus, the beauty of interleaving is that taking a break from one document can be done by working on a different document. "Most mornings I'll spend time on two or three different writing projects," the prolific constitutional law scholar Cass Sunstein has said of his own writing habits. "I like to go back and forth—if I'm stuck on one, I'll jump to the other."

I encourage my students to try something similar. Multitasking, I tell them, remains a bad idea. Study after study has demonstrated that our brains are not good at doing two things simultaneously. But there can be some real benefits to "multiprojecting." When done strategically, interleaving at least one writing assignment with a second might lead to a bonus boost in productivity.

Low-Stakes Practice: Habits and Habitats

On a given day I work on seven different things, probably, in little chunks.

—Actor Seth Rogen, quoted by Jonah Weiner in "Seth Rogen and the Secret to Happiness" (2021)

Below are descriptions of the habits and habitats that professionals from various fields have used to consistently produce original, well-crafted ideas. Which of them involve a form of "interleaving"? (More than one answer may apply.)

A. **Designer Coco Chanel:** "Chanel would set immediately to work on her designs. She refused to use patterns or wooden mannequins, and so would spend long hours draping and pinning fabrics on models, smoking one cigarette after  another, rarely or never sitting down. According to [Chanel's biographer Rhonda Garelick], 'She could remain standing for nine hours at a time, without pausing for a meal or a glass of water—without even a bathroom break, apparently.' She stayed until late in the evening, compelling her employees to hang around with her even after work had ceased, pouring wine and talking nonstop, avoiding for as long as possible the return to her room at the Ritz and to the boredom and loneliness that awaited her there. She worked six days a week, and dreaded Sundays and holidays. As she told one confidant, 'That word, "vacation," makes me sweat.'"

—Mason Currey, *Daily Rituals: Women at Work* (2019)

B. **Harvard Law Professor Cass Sunstein:** "Most days I'll mostly write from 9:30 until noon. There'll be stops and starts, and I'll typically go from one project to another,

depending on how they're going. At the moment I'm working on an article in the general area of behavioral economics and public policy. I'm also working on a magazine piece, on a very different issue. I like to go back and forth—if I'm stuck on one, I'll jump to the other. I'm also working on my next book, which has nothing to do with my current one. I'll turn to that if I feel something's brewing there. Most mornings I'll spend time on two or three different writing projects."

—Cass Sunstein, "How I Write" (2013)

C. **Novelist Haruki Murakami:** "When I'm in writing mode for a novel, I get up at four a.m. and work for five to six hours. In the afternoon, I run for ten kilometers or swim

for fifteen hundred meters (or do both), then I read a bit and listen to some music. I go to bed at nine p.m. I keep to this routine every day without variation. The repetition itself becomes the important thing; it's a form of mesmerism. I mesmerize myself to reach a deeper state of mind. But to hold to such repetition for so long—six months to a year—requires a good amount of mental and physical strength. In that sense, writing a long novel is like survival training. Physical strength is as necessary as artistic sensitivity."

—Haruki Murakami, "The Art of Fiction No. 182" (2004)

D. **Songwriter Bob Dylan:** "It's nice to be able to put yourself in an environment where you can completely accept all the unconscious stuff that comes to you from your inner

workings of your mind. And block yourself off to where you can control it all, take it down. . . . For me, the environment to write the song is extremely important. The environment has to bring something out in me that wants to be brought out. It's a contemplative, reflective thing. . . . People need peaceful, invigorating environments. Stimulating environments."

—Quoted in Paul Zallo, *Songwriters on Songwriting* (1991)

E. **Astrophysicist Sandra Faber:** "It's always been very, very important to me to have a balance between family and work. And I actually think that my work has been helped, especially in those early years, by having to tear myself away and do something different for some hours a day. I actually don't

have that as much now, and I think I'm overall not as efficient per unit of time; I get more done now because I have more hours, but I don't think I'm as efficient as I was back then. So we had a daily routine. I do best when I divide my attention and spend some hours focusing on one thing and then switching attention and doing something different."

—Sandra Faber, "An Interview with Sandra Faber" (2009)

Answer Key

Interleaving

B. **Harvard law professor Cass Sunstein:** Sunstein's habit of switching back and forth between writing projects is a great example of interleaving. (Sunstein's habits were also flagged in the Vocabulary part of the chapter.)

E. **Astrophysicist Sandra Faber:** Unlike Cass Sunstein, Faber doesn't explicitly talk about switching between writing projects. But she does say that "I do best when I divide my attention and spend some hours focusing on one thing and then switching attention and doing something different." This technique can be seen as a form of interleaving.

Not Interleaving

A. **Designer Coco Chanel:** Chanel's uninterrupted approach to work does not involve a form of interleaving.

C. **Novelist Haruki Murakami:** The big, five-to-six-hour blocks of time Murakami reserves for writing do not seem to include opportunities for interleaving. They seem closer to the approach of Coco Chanel than to the approach of Cass Sunstein and Sandra Faber.

E. **Songwriter Bob Dylan:** Dylan focuses on the environmental conditions needed for creativity. The passage doesn't mention anything that resembles interleaving.

High-Stakes Project: Companion Tasks

If I did not have my medical work, I doubt if I could have given my leisure and my spare thoughts to literature.

—Anton Chekhov, Letter to A. S. Surovin (September 11, 1888)

Background

When my students and I design interleaving strategies to help us complete our own high-stakes projects, we try to think carefully about  the type of activities that will work well as complementary tasks. Our goal is the kind of balance that the American writer William Carlos Williams—who was also a practicing physician—found between his daily duties as a doctor and his literary pursuits as a poet. In his 1951 autobiography, Williams notes that he was often asked, "How do you do it? How can you carry on an active business like that and at the same time find time to write? You must be superhuman. You must have at the very least the energy of two men."

His response nicely captures an ideal form of interleaving. "[People] don't grasp that one occupation complements the other, that they are two parts of a whole, that it is not two jobs at all, that one rests the man when the other fatigues him."

A similar view was expressed a bit more cheekily by another famous writer-doctor: the Russian playwright and short-story master Anton Chekhov. "Medicine is my lawful wife, and literature is my mistress," he once explained. "When I get fed up with one, I spend the night with the other. Though it is disorderly, it is less boring this way, and besides, neither of them loses anything through my infidelity."

You don't have to go to the extreme of having two separate professions to benefit from the cognitive shift and restoration that Williams and Chekhov describe. You simply have to find two things that can serve as reciprocally productive pursuits.

Assignment

Consider pairing a project that is in an early stage with a project that is in a much later stage. This combination will give you the chance to switch back and forth between the helpfully different mind-sets of drafting and editing. When you hit a creative block while trying to draft new content, change modes and focus on editing content that already exists. Then, when you hit another creative block, change modes again and focus on drafting new content. Variety, the saying goes, is "the spice of life." But it can also be the catalyst for new ideas and insights.

Be aware, though, that your transitions between drafting and editing won't always be seamless and that you'll be particularly vulnerable to "attention residue," which is a term the management professor Sophie Leroy of the University of Washington coined to describe when "part of our attention is focused on another task instead of being fully devoted to the current task that needs to be performed." Think of a parent who, having just sent an important work email, continues to ruminate about it while trying to read their five-year-old a bedtime story. Or consider a college student who struggles to refocus on their calculus homework after checking what some friends just posted on Instagram. A divided brain is rarely an efficient or optimally receptive brain.

That said, an increasing amount of evidence shows that strategic task-switching can lead to something that seems particularly useful to both editors and advocates: enhanced creativity. A team of researchers at Columbia Business School, for example, found that participants who alternated between two tasks produced ideas that were both more novel and more flexible. "Setting aside tasks facilitates creativity," the team explains in the *Journal of Organizational Behavior and Human Decision Processes*, "because breaks reduce cognitive fixation, which is a necessary step for generating creative output." Several other studies have come to similar conclusions. They don't deny that focusing on one thing at a time is good. They simply suggest we consider rotating what that one thing will be.

So take a shot at picking a separate project to serve as a companion task to your high-stakes one. When my students and I use this technique, we sometimes think in terms of the six-minute increments in which many lawyers bill their time. A good companion task is a piece of editing (or proofreading) you could do in six, twelve, eighteen, or even twenty-four minutes. Anything beyond that and I start to worry that the companion task may start to sap the energy you'll need when you return to your primary task. The point is to combat cognitive fixation. You don't want to overreach and induce cognitive exhaustion. Nobody should take a break from working on their dissertation by writing a second one.

* * *

Here are a few options of primary and companion tasks to give you a sense of the combinatorial possibilities. Mix and match in whatever way you think will be useful to you, although certainly feel free to come up with different items for each category. Think of yourself as an executive chef designing a dinner menu. Which appetizers and sides go best with the main course? Don't serve steak with steak.

Primary Task (Draft)	Foil Task (Edit)
A legal brief you haven't started	A legal brief you're close to finishing
A blog post for this coming week	A blog post from last week
A syllabus for a new course	A syllabus from a course you'll be teaching again
An important email to your boss	A memo a coworker asked you to review
A novel	A short story, essay, or poem
A cover letter	Your résumé

PART II

Words. Words. I play with words, hoping that some combination, even a chance combination, will say what I want.

—Doris Lessing, *The Golden Notebook* (1994)

PREVIOUSLY ON

I want to start this section with a little review of the last section. In my classes, we call this "Previously On" because it resembles the recap that TV shows give at the beginning of a new episode. Sometimes, students take their note-books out during Previously On and write down what they remember about the concepts covered in earlier sessions. Other times, they work through a set of short questions and exercises designed to help them reconnect with the material.

In both cases, the process has at least two benefits. First, like the TV version of Previously On, the class version creates a helpful layer of Velcro in your brain. Before new material latches on—whether in a show, a book, or some other medium—it can be helpful to go over familiar material. Context helps with comprehension.

The second benefit of Previously On is that it promotes an import-ant aspect of learning: retrieval. Passive consumption is not a great way to educate yourself and acquire new skills. To really improve and get knowledge to stick, you need to make sure your brain knows how to find, sort, and activate that knowledge.

We discussed the importance of this retrieval process in Chapter 2, when we learned about the idea of "desirable difficulties" developed by the UCLA psychologist Robert Bjork. Here's a sentence from that chapter. See if you can jump-start your own retrieval practice by guessing what goes in each blank.

1. "When we access things from our memory, we do more than reveal it's there. It's not like a playback. What we retrieve becomes more retrievable in the future. Provided the retrieval succeeds, the more _____ the retrieval, the more beneficial it is."

   A. simple and painless
   B. difficult and involved
   C. high-stakes and interleaved
   D. low-stakes and conceptual

Now try the same thing with a sentence from Chapter 1.

2. "You might even think of this use of empathy in _____ terms. It's goal-oriented compassion. The more accurately you imagine what it's like to be the people you are trying to persuade, the more likely you'll be to craft a message that successfully addresses their particular concerns and preferences."

   A. habitual
   B. advocacy
   C. procrastination
   D. strategic

To test how you did, check out the answers on the next page. As a bit of extra review, you might also take a shot at quickly summarizing the distinctions we drew between the following labels:

- Editing vs. proofreading
- Teachers vs. readers

Of course, if you'd rather move on to fresh material, that's fine too. Simply turn to Chapter 3, where we'll encounter a new, beneficial category of edits: anticipatory edits.

Answer Key

Question 1

B. "When we access things from our memory, we do more than reveal it's there. It's not like a playback. What we retrieve becomes more retrievable in the future. Provided the retrieval succeeds, the more <u>difficult and involved</u> the retrieval, the more beneficial it is."

Question 2

D. "You might even think of this use of empathy in <u>strategic</u> terms. It's goal-oriented compassion. The more accurately you imagine what it's like to be the people you are trying to persuade, the more likely you'll be to craft a message that successfully addresses their particular concerns and preferences."

Distinctions

Editing vs. Proofreading. "Proofreading involves catching typos and fixing formatting. It cultivates a host of admirable qualities—patience, thoroughness, attention to detail—but it doesn't require a whole lot of imagination.

Editing, on the other hand, is a fundamentally creative act. Good editors don't just see the sentence that was written. They see the sentence that *might* have been written. They know how to spot words that shouldn't be included and summon up ones that haven't yet appeared. Their value comes not just from preventing mistakes but from discovering new ways to improve a piece's style, structure, and overall impact."

Teachers vs. Readers. "A lot of us have spent many years in an educational system in which people—namely, our teachers—were paid to read our writing and care about the ideas we communicate.

If you're still in school, it's worth considering what is going to happen when you graduate and enter a world in which that kind of subsidized attention is no longer available. How might your current approach to writing need to change once it is no longer a given that anyone will be interested in what you have to say?"

CHAPTER 3

Anticipatory Edits

It is better for your career if you fix your own
mistakes; I do not enjoy fixing them for you.

—Mark Herrmann, *The Curmudgeon's*
Guide to Practicing Law (2006)

Good writing, I often tell my students, is "anticipating the edits of your boss." I then clarify that the definition of "boss" in that statement is intentionally expansive.

A supervisor at work can count. A teacher in school can count. So can a particularly valued customer or client. The key is to start thinking about two things:

- The actual people who are going to review your writing
- The likely changes they'll make to it

By implementing those changes yourself—*before* the document ever hits your boss's desk or inbox—you can save everybody a lot of time and cognitive effort. I doubt people will hold that against you.

A. Targeted Foresight

One way to think about anticipating the edits of your boss is to view the process as a form of targeted foresight. You need to make informed predictions about a particular person's future revisions and then adjust your current draft accordingly.

Studying past revisions can help. So can talking to people who have worked with your boss before. Discovering someone's pet peeves through a little research and networking is a lot less painful than discovering someone's pet peeves only because you irritatingly violate them.

You'll also want to build the capacity to do something that is crucial in many professional and academic settings, particularly ones in which the organizational hierarchy means that what you will write will ultimately be reviewed, signed, and filed by a superior: adapt to somebody else's preferences. Interdependent writing doesn't work so well when what goes into the system has to be completely redone by the person at the other end of the supply chain.

A federal judge, for example, once offered the following succinct explanation when I asked her what went wrong with a former clerk she regretted hiring: "He never learned to write like me." The clerk was bright. The clerk was motivated. The clerk had been educated at one of the top law schools in the country. His fatal flaw, however, was failing to develop a skill that is unfortunately as undertaught as it is professionally valuable: ventriloquism. Your job as a law clerk is to write in the voice of your judge, just like your job as an associate is to write in the voice of whichever partner is giving you assignments. These gigs are not platforms for self-expression.

I say that as someone who took an embarrassingly long time to understand that a lot of the writing I would be doing in the professional world would be for other people. I didn't immediately grasp the value you can add by knowing how to draft a document (or even just an email) that matches how your boss would compose it themselves. It wasn't until I started my own clerkship that I finally had what would turn out to be an important epiphany. I realized that anticipatory edits are among the most efficient—and the most considerate—edits you can make.

B. A Tale of Two Judges

The special circumstances of my clerkship greatly accelerated my sorely needed awakening. I worked for two judges at once.

Both judges were excellent writers. But they were also very *different* writers. One of them, whom we'll call "Judge A," drafted opinions using WordPerfect, a software application I had never used before. The other, whom we'll call "Judge B," preferred Microsoft Word.

Although I fortunately already had a lot of experience with Microsoft Word, having to divide my digital loyalty between that program and WordPerfect definitely affected my cumulative proficiency. The more I learned about WordPerfect, the more I forgot about Microsoft

Word. I was like someone who, in trying to speak a second language, sometimes forgets how to communicate in their first.

Another difference between the two judges was their approach to making revisions. Judge A handwrote every comment in an exquisite red script that often rose to the level of calligraphy. Never have crossed-out commas looked so classy. Judge B's edits were also classy, but they were generally generated electronically. "Track Changes"— not a red pen—was the delivery method of choice.

Even the things the two judges shared, such as an admirable commitment to the precise use of language, manifested themselves in separate ways. Perched on Judge A's desk was a bobblehead doll of the legal writing expert and lexicographer Bryan Garner. Perched on Judge B's was a sign that signaled a similar fastidiousness, but in a more biting manner. It read, "I am silently correcting your grammar."

Along these same lines, although my decision to include the word "persnickety" received high praise in a draft I submitted to Judge A, I knew better than to try that kind of thing with Judge B. In Judge B's view, being clear meant being conversational. And when's the last time you heard someone say "persnickety" out loud, let alone over a cup of coffee?

C. Linguistic Flexibility

Having to regularly toggle between my judges' parallel sets of expectations and preferences wasn't easy. But it was a tremendous form of training. Forced to figure out how to write in two distinct voices— neither of which was my own—I developed a helpful amount of linguistic flexibility. I had to adjust to each judge's approach to word choice. I had to adjust to each judge's approach to word order. And I certainly had to adjust to each judge's approach to word prohibitions.

Judge A, for example, subscribed to the view that the word "which" should not be used to introduce what's known as a "restrictive" or "essential" clause—basically a clause that provides important identifying information about the noun that precedes it.

- **Prohibited:** "The four products <u>which</u> the plaintiff bought were all defective."
- **Proper:** "The four products <u>that</u> the plaintiff bought were all defective."

This prohibition even extended to sentences quoted from other sources. Judge A would use corrective brackets to switch the offending *which* to a much more palatable *that*.

- **Original Version:** "The four products <u>which</u> the plaintiff bought were all defective."
- **Judge A Version:** "The four products [<u>that</u>] the plaintiff bought were all defective."

Anticipating this edit, I dutifully started doing the exact same thing. But only for Judge A.

That's because Judge B didn't feel as strongly about *which* and *that*. So the Judge B version of me didn't either. I didn't modify quotations. I didn't use corrective brackets. Instead, I focused on a distinction that mattered a lot more to Judge B: *since* vs. *because*.

A lot of people use *since* and *because* interchangeably—to signal causation.

- **Option 1:** "<u>Since</u> the four products that the plaintiff bought were all defective, she returned them."
- **Option 2:** "<u>Because</u> the four products that the plaintiff bought were all defective, she returned them."*

---

* Both judges were fine with starting a sentence with "Because."

43

Not Judge B. To Judge B, the word "since" didn't signal causation. It signaled chronology.

- **Prohibited:** "<u>Since</u> the four products that the plaintiff bought were all defective, she returned them."
- **Preferred:** "<u>Since</u> buying the four products this morning, she has already returned three of them."

Judge B actually highlighted this semantic difference during my interview for the clerkship position. The difference then surfaced again in a follow-up email I received from Judge B a few days later. Pasted into the email was a sentence I had written in one of our earlier correspondences. I had used *since* in the prohibited way.

Given that I had already been offered the job at this point, Judge B simply underlined the infraction and added the following admonition, playfully raising doubts about the wisdom of deciding to hire me: "I may have to reconsider."

D. Compositional Humility

Remembering whether your boss prefers *that* over *which* or *because* over *since* might not seem like the hardest of tasks. But the simple act of taking that kind of preference into consideration can help remind you that a good deal of writing is coproduced.

To get a sense of what I mean, check out the "Acknowledgments" section of your favorite nonfiction book. The number of people whom the author thanks is a good illustration of just how many minds and forms of support go into putting together a quality piece of work.

Pieces of fiction don't typically include an "Acknowledgments" section, but that doesn't mean the world's greatest novels, plays, and short stories were brought into the world unassisted. Tolstoy had an editor. Hemingway had an editor. Even Jane Austen—about whom her brother Henry once said, "Everything came finished from her

44

pen"—had an editor, according to recent archival research by Kathryn Sutherland of Oxford University.

Or think of the best individual advocate you know. Chances are they have an assistant, friend, or spouse who doubles as a darn good proofreader and sounding board. Few things worth reading are written alone.

Yet even though writing can often feel like a team sport, it is important to keep in mind that when you're just starting out in your career, your position on that team is unlikely to be quarterback, pitcher, or any other high-status spot. You're a role-player. Your value comes from helping other people shine. Which means you have to learn to contribute—and compromise—accordingly. Self-aggrandizement is rarely a good career move.

Instead, try to cultivate a trait that nicely complements the linguistic flexibility we already mentioned: compositional humility.

In my own writing, for example, I don't follow Judge A's prohibition against *which* or Judge B's prohibition against *since*. I've seen too many skilled writers ignore both of these "rules" to think that either is an unbreakable mandate.

But the writing I did for Judge A and Judge B wasn't *my* writing. It was their writing. My signature didn't appear at the bottom of any document we filed. My public reputation wasn't on the line.

Neither of them hired me to craft sentences and paragraphs in my own distinctive voice. They hired me to craft sentences and paragraphs in *their* distinctive voices. When I did my job right, I channeled their words, their syntax, their refreshingly unique way of explaining why they've made a particular decision. I channeled, in short, the judges themselves—idiosyncratic prohibitions and all.

* * *

Now that I am a law professor, I get to hire the student equivalent of clerks: research assistants. We talk about anticipatory edits a lot, especially when it comes to improving the quality of the pieces I publish. The students don't really take on the drafting responsibilities that many clerks are assigned. But it has been fun to see them embrace the idea of anticipatory edits in other ways.

Perhaps my favorite comment of all time was when a research assistant who had worked with me for multiple semesters changed the wording of two of my sentences and then left the following note: "I tried to make the sentences sound more like you."

I love that. Someone completely different from me—different age; different upbringing; different set of preferences, priorities, and overall life experiences—was able to do a better job of making sure I sounded like me than I could. That gives me a whole new level of anticipatory edits to shoot for: anticipating the edits of myself.

Low-Stakes Practice: Pet Peeves

As both devoted reader and literary practitioner, Stephen King has pet peeves worth appreciating. He passionately hates adverbs, which means that "He hates adverbs" would be a better way of saying so. Ditto for loathing passive constructions in place of active ones, in a point that he makes with typical no-nonsense bluntness. "I think unsure writers also feel the passive voice somehow lends their work authority, perhaps even a quality of majesty," he says. (He also prefers a simple "says" or "said" to fancier forms of dialogue attribution.)

—Janet Maslin, "How to Write (If You're Stephen King)" (2000)

Background

For many lawyers, the idea of "anticipating the edits of your boss" has an important corollary: "anticipating the edits of the judge who will decide your case." A motion, brief, or contract full of the judge's pet peeves faces a steep uphill battle.

To help publicize widely held pet peeves, the legal writing expert Ross Guberman surveyed over one thousand state and federal judges in 2018. The good news, he explains in an article for *Litigation* magazine, is that judges "agree on much more than many litigators might think, and I found no major differences based on region or type of court." The bad news: "Almost every filing I see violates the wish lists of the judges I surveyed."

Guberman turns the results from the survey into actionable pieces of advice. He begins with a warning about the often-unhelpful labels lawyers use to identify the parties in their cases. "For starters, watch how you name names. Use the parties' names rather than their procedural affiliation. Prefer words to unfamiliar acronyms, even if the word or phrase is longer. Avoid defining obvious terms like 'FBI' and 'Ford Motor Company.'"

He then provides a few choice quotations from judges themselves, as a way to capture and individualize their collective annoyance.

- "I absolutely detest party labels (plaintiff, debtor, creditor, etc.). Name names, for God's sake!"
- "Don't use 'plaintiff,' 'defendant,' 'appellant,' or 'appellee' in the brief because we may forget who's who. Instead, use names for individuals and business titles for companies."
- "Avoid defining obvious terms. If a party is Apple Computer Corp., why include the parenthetical ('Apple')? If the plaintiff's name is Henry Jackson and he's the only Jackson in the case, why the need to identify him as Henry Jackson ('Jackson')? If the case is about one and only one contract, when first identifying it, why the need for (the 'Contract')?"

Later in the essay, Guberman follows up these general pronouncements with comments from judges on specific words and phrases they'd like to see permanently deleted.

- "Don't use words like 'wherefore,' 'heretofore,' 'hereinafter' that aren't commonly used in everyday language."
- "Don't use 'at that time' for 'when.'"
- "Don't use 'prior to' for 'before' or 'subsequent to' for 'after.'"
- "I don't like unnecessary Latin phrases like 'inter alia.'"
- "'Aforesaid,' 'heretofore,' etc. are all pretty much empty and add nothing. Same with 'said,' as in the 'said contract was signed at the said meeting.'"
- "I cannot stand 'As such' used as a synonym for 'Therefore.'"
- "I loathe the word 'utilize.'"

Assignment

Even if the writing you do each day doesn't typically involve judges, Guberman's list may still be useful. It identifies a host of stylistic choices—as well as a broader tone of pretentiousness—that can really irk people.

So feel free to consult it as you complete the Low-Stakes Practice exercise for this chapter, which is to make your own list of pet peeves. Giving some thought to what bugs you when you see it in other people's writing will, I hope, make you more careful about causing similar levels of irritation in somebody else.

As additional inspiration, here are two more sample sets of pet peeves. The first comes from a group of professional copy editors Emmy Favilla, the author of *A World without Whom: The Official Guide to Language in the Buzzfeed Age*, interviewed at the annual conference for the Society for Editing in 2017:

- **Redundancy:** "Skip 'reasons why.' 'Reasons' are sufficient!"
- **Punctuation:** "Using en dashes, em dashes, and hyphens interchangeably."
- **Whom:** "Let's get rid of 'whom.' 'Who' works fine. And no one uses [whom] correctly anyway."
- **Misused Phrases:** "Would of? No." (The preferred phrase is "Would have.") "Try and . . ." (The preferred phrase is "Try to . . .")
- **Prepositions:** "Your teachers didn't know what they were talking about. You can end a sentence with a preposition if you want to."

The second set also comes from a group of copy editors, but these copy editors primarily focus on science writing. Put together by the Council of Science Editors in an article called "Science Editors and Their Pet Peeves," the list touches on everything from misplaced modifiers to superfluous words to ignoring length requirements.

- **Misplaced Modifiers:** "When a phrase isn't next to the noun it modifies and sounds like it modifies something else—that's something I'm a stickler for."
- **Superfluous Words:** "For Carol Kornblith, an author's editor at the Mayo Foundation, one pet peeve is the useless phrase 'the truth of the matter is.'"
- **Ignoring Length Requirements:** "When *Science News* articles must be cut drastically to meet length requirements, editor Julie Miller said, they can lose coherence. Although journal articles are much longer than the pieces that appear in *Science News*, Stephen Rachlin said length requirements are still a problem. 'I give an absolute space limitation, and the number of people who follow the guidelines is small indeed.'"

It's worth ending with a final catchall pet peeve from Diana Lutz, the editor of the children's magazine *Muse*. She offers a nice bit of appreciation for those writers who embrace the idea of anticipatory edits and try to reduce the amount of cleanup work she has to do. "All [my] pet peeves can be subsumed under one pet peeve: writers who do only half the work, leaving me to either kill or rescue the article. As the editor, I have the opportunity to compare their performance with that of the dedicated few who pour in time and effort and work not until the money runs out, but until the thing is done right. Those people have my undying gratitude."

High-Stakes Project: It's Not about You

I could spend an hour with Ben dictating my arguments on a subject and count on getting a draft a few days later that not only captured my voice but also channeled something more essential: my bedrock view of the world, and sometimes even my heart.

> —Barack Obama, describing Ben Rhodes, his Deputy National Security Advisor for Strategic Communications and Speechwriting, in Obama's memoir *A Promised Land* (2020)

Background

In the Vocabulary section of this chapter, we learned about the compositional humility required when writing as part of a team. We also learned that this type of humility is even more important when your role on that team is more of a supporting player—or if your job specifically involves crafting sentences in someone else's voice. (That was the position I was in when I worked as a law clerk for Judge A and Judge B.)

This next exercise gives you a chance to try something that I found to be enormously helpful both during my time in that position and while working in many other collaborative contexts: making an "It's Not about You" list.

Assignment

Step 1: Identify your boss—at least for the project you are currently working on. This person might be your direct supervisor. This person might be your client. This person might be anyone who will at some point review your work and approve the final product. Possibilities include:
- the partner you are working under at a law firm
- the principal investigator on your research grant
- the editor of a magazine, blog, or academic journal where you hope to publish something you wrote
- your thesis advisor

Step 2: Think of some writing issues about which you and your boss might differ. Do you each agree that it is okay to start sentences with *And* or *But?* Are you both open to occasionally splitting infinitives? How about the length and variety of your paragraphs? Do yours match up with theirs, or will some significant adjustments need to be made?

The most direct way to obtain this information is to ask your boss. But there are indirect options as well, particularly if you're nervous about taking up their time or unsure about how the conversation might go.

Perhaps the least intrusive method is to simply check out some of your boss's own writing. Even from a small sample, you can learn a lot about their approach to tone, organization, evidence, examples, concision, and a host of other topics. When I was working for Judge A and Judge B, for instance, I would try to read at least one judicial opinion by them every morning, before I started my own drafts. The extra exposure had both a macro-level and a micro-level payoff.

The macro-level payoff was that I gradually started to internalize the rhythms of each judge's thought process and modes of expression, sort of like an actor who immerses themselves in the speech patterns of the real-life figure he is hired to portray. "On any given day," the three-time Oscar-winner Daniel Day-Lewis said of the year he spent training to inhabit the role of Abraham Lincoln in 2013, "I learned quite a number of pieces of Lincoln's writing, so that I could live with those every day and speak them every day." Leonardo DiCaprio

took similar steps when getting ready to play the stockbroker Jordan Belfort in *The Wolf of Wall Street*.

The micro-level payoff was that I was able to catalogue the differences between my writing and the judges' writing. I compared the frequency with which I used semicolons to the frequency with which they used semicolons. I compared the places where I included headings (and subheadings) to the places where they included headings (and subheadings). And I definitely compared our respective vocabulary choices, having once heard a different judge say the following about one of his clerks, in a frustrated—even exhausted—kind of way: "He keeps using words I need to google."

Step 3: When you have at least three categories of comparison, take out a piece of paper and make three columns. At the top of one column, put your name. At the top of the next, put your boss's name. Then fill in where each of you stands on the writing issues in your categories.

	Patrick	Judge A
Starts sentences with "And" or "But"	Yes	Yes
Reserves "which" for nonrestrictive clauses	No	Yes
Uses the Oxford comma	Yes	Yes

Step 4: Now comes the "It's Not about You" part. Circle any category in which you and your boss differ. (For me, that would be the "which" issue.) Then write in the margins, in a way that will become a mental reminder the next time you have to decide whether to follow your way of handling the issue or your boss's way, "It's Not about You." If it helps, specify the project:

- "This report is not about you."

- "This legal brief is not about you."
- "This research is not about you."

I don't mean that you're not the subject of the document, although that is likely true as well. I mean that your preferences, opinions, and interests don't necessarily get priority.

CHAPTER 4

The Animal Farm Principle

Eventually I realized that I was clearer-headed, more confident and generally more intelligent in the morning. The habit of getting up early, which I had formed when the children were young, now became my choice. I am not very bright or very witty or very inventive after the sun goes down.

—Toni Morrison, "The Art of Fiction No. 134" (1993)

There are a lot of really good sentences in the book *Animal Farm*, George Orwell's allegorical account of totalitarianism in which two ambitious pigs—Napoleon and Snowball—lead the rest of the farm animals in a revolt against their human overseers. But perhaps its most famous sentence is the following:

All animals are equal, but some animals are more equal than others.

As satire, the sentence offers a biting critique of a falsely fair system. If, however, we slightly modify the sentence, we can get a helpful way to think about time management, particularly when it comes to structuring our writing sessions:

All <u>hours</u> are equal, but some hours are more equal than others.

On one level, yes, all hours are equal. They each have sixty minutes. Yet on a different level, some hours are definitely *more equal*, depending on your own habits, preferences, and external obligations. The hour between 7:00 a.m. and 8:00 a.m., for example, is worth a lot more to a morning person in terms of productivity than it is to a night owl—just as the hour right after lunch may be a mental dead zone for some people but the precise spot when others finally hit their cognitive stride. As the Berkeley psychologist Matthew Walker points out in *Why We Sleep*, both early risers and late risers can be highly effective. They just need to be allowed to operate according to their own optimally efficient schedules.

With that in mind, take a moment to think of your own preferences and patterns. During which hours do you produce your best work? Before 10:00 a.m.? After 2:00 p.m.? Somewhere close to when the sun starts to set?

Or perhaps you're like people as different as the Pulitzer Prize–winning novelist Michael Chabon and the billionaire investor Carl Icahn. Their brains are apparently still cranking long after most folks have gone to bed. "My natural rhythm is to work at night, stay up late and to sleep late," Chabon told an interviewer for the *Los Angeles Times* back in 2009. "I can get more writing done between midnight and 1 o'clock in the morning than at any other hour of the day." Icahn, a champion of shareholder activism, takes a similarly nocturnal approach. If you want to close a deal with him, the business journalists Caleb Melby and Heather Perlberg report, you may need to adjust your internal alarm clock.

* * *

Channeling the return-on-investment mentality of a financier like Carl Icahn might not be a bad idea as you think about which of your own hours are *more equal* than others. In other words, treat those hours like extremely valuable assets.

Don't trade them away or let any sit idle. Instead, try to put as many to use on your most important projects, whether professional, personal, or some combination of both.

A resource that might help is the book *Art Thinking: How to Carve Out Creative Space in a World of Schedules, Budgets, and Bosses*. The book was written by Amy Whitaker, who teaches at NYU and holds an interesting pair of degrees. She has an MFA in painting from University College London and an MBA in strategy from the Yale School of Management. So she's artistic, but she's also really pragmatic—an intermingling of mindsets that animates the whole book.

"*Art Thinking* is about how to construct a life of originality and meaning within the real constraints of the market economy," she explains in the introductory chapter. "It is about how to make space for vulnerability and the possibility of failure within the world of work, with its very real and structural pressures to get things done, to win praise and adulation, and to contribute to bottom-line growth."

One of Whitaker's specific pieces of advice is to regularly set aside "studio time," which she defines as a time to indulge your curiosity. "Do anything you want with that time," she clarified in an interview with the *Financial Times* in 2016. "The point is to give yourself ritualized time and space to learn and do."

For Whitaker, an important characteristic of studio time is that it be a safe place to experiment and fail—so the concept might at first seem better suited to the Low-Stakes Practice sections of this book. But I've found that the idea of consistently building in protected amounts of time for yourself can help with high-stakes projects as well. I know lawyers who use versions of studio time to work on really important briefs and contracts, even going so far as to schedule recurring meetings with themselves to make sure they have sufficiently big chunks of the day blocked off. I know judges, professors, and CEOs who do something similar.

Each of them is intentional about what the Georgetown computer scientist Cal Newport calls *deep work*: "Professional activities performed in a state of distraction-free concentration that push your cognitive capabilities to their limit. These efforts create new value, improve your skill, and are hard to replicate."

Newport contrasts *deep work* with *shallow work*, which he defines as "noncognitively demanding, logistical-style tasks, often performed while distracted. These efforts tend to not create much new value in the world and are easy to replicate."

It would be a waste to use your studio time on shallow work. You can do shallow work between meetings, while commuting, maybe even while waiting in line. But for your really hard, high-value projects, consider Whitaker's idea, even if just to set up a mental studio.

You don't need a smock. You don't need an easel. You simply need a consistent commitment to focusing your attention—and your schedule—on something that is important and, ideally, edifying.

Perhaps that something will even turn out to be a piece of writing as insightful and well crafted as *Animal Farm* itself. That would be a nice, much more positive way of being Orwellian.*

---

* In *Daily Rituals: How Artists Work*, Mason Currey includes the following description of Orwell's own preferred writing schedule. It was helped by a switch from an exhausting set of teaching jobs to a less taxing and more flexible part-time position at a London bookshop: "The post at Booklovers' Corner proved an ideal fit for the thirty-one-year-old bachelor. Waking at 7:00, Orwell went to open the shop at 8:45 and stayed there for an hour. Then he had free time until 2:00, when he would return to the shop and work until 6:30. This left him almost four and a half hours of writing time in the morning and early afternoon, which, conveniently, were the times that he was most mentally alert."

Low-Stakes Practice: The Silver Lining of Fatigue

Proclaimed the time was neither wrong nor right
I have been one acquainted with the night.

—Robert Frost, "Acquainted with the Night" (1928)

Read the following collection of daily writing routines. Then, remembering the "Animal Farm Principle"—which encourages us to identify the most productive and valuable parts of our day—pick the description that best captures the set of hours that are, to you, *more equal* than others.

There's no right answer to this question. It's simply a chance for you to reflect on your own preferences and then identify with a writer who shares them:

- **Early Morning:** "When I am working on a book or a story, I write every morning as soon after first light as possible. There is no one to disturb you, and it is cool or cold and you come to your work and warm as you write."
  —Ernest Hemingway, "The Art of Fiction No. 21" (1958)

- **Midmorning:** "I'm always in a hurry to get going, though in general I dislike starting the day. I first have tea and then, at about ten o'clock, I get under way and work until one."
  —Simone de Beauvoir, "The Art of Fiction No. 35" (1965)

- **Afternoon:** "Work on section in hand, following plan of section scrupulously. No intrusions, no diversions. Write to finish one section at a time, for good and all."
  —Henry Miller, *Henry Miller on Writing* (1964)

- **Night:** "I write this from a swivel chair at 4:17 a.m. Twitter has gone quiet. There is darkness for miles. I can hear a watch tick. It's the longest night of the year, and if I time things carefully, I could avoid daylight for 48 hours. What's more, research suggests it won't just be me. There's a mislaid family of readers and writers at night, and at this hour there's nothing else to do but search for them.

Robert Frost was up late. So were Delmore Schwartz, Allen Ginsberg, Pablo Neruda, Charles Dickens and Carol Ann Duffy."

—Matt Shoard, "Writing at Night" (2010)

In *Air & Light & Time & Space: How Successful Academics Write*, Helen Sword of the University of Auckland in New Zealand shares her findings from interviews with an international collection of one hundred accomplished researchers and professors. No consensus on the "perfect time of day" emerged.

Some people, like the psychologist Alison Gopnik, said that their most productive hours are in the afternoon. "I'm not very good first thing in the morning," she confessed, "so I like to do not-so-challenging things then. But between three and seven p.m., between afternoon tea and dinner, that's when the best writing comes." Others, like the physicist Sun Kwok, prefer the evening. "I write in the evenings, and it keeps my sanity. After these days of meetings and dealings with budgets and this boring stuff, there is a total switching of gears."

Another perspective to consider belongs to Leonard Mlodinow, a theoretical physicist who has published several best-selling books on math and science and also produced a number of TV scripts in Hollywood for shows such as *MacGyver*, *Night Court*, and *Star Trek: The Next Generation*. In his 2018 book *Elastic: Unlocking Your Brain's Ability to Embrace Change*, Mlodinow describes "the silver lining of fatigue." Citing research done by a team of French scientists—as well as an experiment conducted by the psychologists Mareike Weith and Rose Zacks—Mlodinow points out that although it is often wise to reserve rigorous, analytic thinking for when our minds are fresh and alert, our capacity for creativity may be highest when our minds are a bit hazy or even when we feel "burnt out."

Mlodinow's own experience provides a helpful example. Confessing that he is a little slow and befuddled at the start of each day, he says that he generally does his best science at night. It's only then that he has the mental energy needed to methodically work through academic papers such as "A Semi-Classical Perturbation Theory for Quantum Mechanics" and "Quantization of Electrodynamics in Nonlinear Dialectic Media." And yet he "noticed long ago that I'm more successful at *writing* during that foggy and otherwise useless morning time."

His big takeaway: "I've learned to listen to my rhythms—that some activities are best done when I still have sleep in my eyes, and others after the weight of the day has painted dark circles beneath them."

High-Stakes Project: Calendar Sync

It's 5:00 p.m. at my house in Nederland, Colorado, and I remember that I have a 6:00–7:30 p.m. team meeting. I need to plan the family dinner around it. I head to the kitchen to prep a chicken and vegetables, timing them so they will roast and rest during my meeting and we can sit down to eat as soon as I am done. In Grand Rapids, several team members will join the meeting at 8:00 p.m., after their dinners and evening plans. In Hong Kong, it will be 8:00 a.m. and Elise and Yushi will either be at the studio or still at home, since the train commute can take a while. In San Francisco, Meike will likely call in from the Coalesse Studio. The meeting today is "no Paris" since it is 2:00 a.m. there and Beatriz will be sleeping.
—Donna Flynn, "Managing a Team across 5 Time Zones" (2014)

Background

This chapter has primarily focused on applying the Animal Farm Principle to your own schedule. But given how collaborative many high-stakes projects are, you might also want to consider applying the principle to the schedules of key members of your team. Maybe you've partnered with a coauthor. Maybe you need to conduct interviews. Maybe you plan to incorporate time-sensitive information from surveys, lab results, or commissioned research.

Or maybe you simply need to accommodate the daily routines of the people (and pets) with whom you share a living space or office. Whatever the calculation, picking your best hours could very well involve some outside inputs.

Assignment

Make a list of up to three people whose work habits and life rhythms will likely affect the success of your high-stakes project. What do you know about their preferred calendars? Are they early birds? Are they night owls? Is the best time to catch them not during but *outside* of normal business hours?

You might also take into account any special pressures on their current calendar. Babies, vacations, important deadlines on other projects—each of these factors could influence, if only in the short term, which hours they consider "more equal than others." The better you can sync your schedule with theirs, the less organizational friction you'll create. It is tough to get people to help you when you sabotage plans they've tried hard to protect.

PART III

*A wonderful thing about writing
is that you can revise.*

—Bernard Malamud, *The Tenants* (1971)

PREVIOUSLY ON

Now that we have covered the major concepts in Part II, it's again time for "Previously On," that helpful chance to reflect on what we've learned and prepare ourselves for new content. Research suggests that taking this type of step really improves learning and retention. Ulrich Boser, the author of *Learn Better*, summed up the findings well in an interview with the *Atlantic* back in 2017. "Re-reading and high-lighting are particularly ineffective [forms of studying]. They're just passive, and you are just kind of skimming that material. It makes you feel better. You feel comfortable with the material, but you don't really know the material. Doing things that are a little bit more difficult, that require you to really make connections, is a better way to learn. [You might] explain things to yourself, [or] simply quiz yourself. If you're preparing for a meeting, you'd be much better off just putting the material away and just asking yourself questions."

Boser then elaborates on what is so helpful about trying to explain new materials to yourself and also trying to teach them to others. "Self-explaining has a lot of evidence. You're explaining why things might be interconnected, and why they matter, and those meaningful distinctions between the two of them. The other thing that's partic-ularly helpful about teaching other people is that you have to think about what is confusing about something, and how you'd explain that in a simpler way, and so that makes you shift the way that you're thinking about a certain topic."

So that's what I want you to do with the three concepts listed below: review each of them by performing some self-explaining.

- Anticipatory Edits
- The Animal Farm Principle
- Studio Time

Even better, try to teach them to a friend or family member. A clear indication that you know you have done a good job understanding something is when you can get another person to understand it too.

Note: If you need a quick refresher on any of the three concepts, take a look at the "Explanatory Excerpts" section on the next page. It contains reminder passages from the relevant chapters.

Explanatory Excerpts

Anticipatory Edits: "One way to think about anticipating the edits of your boss is to view the process as a form of targeted foresight. You need to make informed predictions about a particular person's future revisions and then adjust your current draft accordingly." (See Pg. 40.)

The Animal Farm Principle: "On one level, yes, all hours are equal. They each have sixty minutes. Yet on a different level, some hours are definitely *more equal*, depending on your own habits, preferences, and external obligations. The hour between 7:00 a.m. and 8:00 a.m., for example, is worth a lot more to a morning person in terms of productivity than it is to a night owl—just as the hour right after lunch may be a mental dead zone for some people but the precise spot when others finally hit their cognitive stride." (See Pg. 56.)

Studio Time: "The point is to give yourself ritualized time and space to learn and do." (See Pg. 58.)

CHAPTER 5

Map to a Decision

[The University of Michigan philosophy professor Elizabeth Anderson] takes great pleasure in arranging information in useful forms; if she weren't a philosopher, she thinks, she'd like to be a map maker, or a curator of archeological displays in museums.

—Nathan Heller, "The Philosopher Redefining Equality" (2018)

Writers are mapmakers, especially when it comes to persuading people to make a certain decision.

Maybe the decision is about whether to rule in your client's favor. A legal brief creates a map to do that. Maybe the decision is about whether to invest in a business. A prospectus creates a map to do that. Or maybe it's about something more individual, like whether you deserve a spot in a particular school, program, or organization. Think here of admissions essays, cover letters, and job applications. The more clearly you can lay out the steps necessary to reach a specific conclusion, the more successful you're likely to be. It's tough to arrive at a destination that is impossible to find.

To push this connection between writing and mapping a little further, let's look at an experiment mentioned in the best-selling book *Switch* by two brothers—Chip Heath, who teaches at the Stanford Business School, and Dan Heath, who teaches at Duke. The experiment involved a food drive on a college campus. The point was to see if small changes in the way the food drive was advertised could increase the amount of donations.

One announcement for the food drive contained generic instructions to bring a can of food to where the drive was being held, which was a well-known place on campus—something like the student union. The second announcement included additional details. It switched the phrase "can of food," which is pretty general, to the more specific phrase "can of beans." It also suggested that the recipients think of a time they were going to be near the drop-off spot, the hope being that not having to take a separate trip would make it easier for them to make a donation. But the smartest thing the second announcement contained was the following: an actual map to the drop-off spot.

It's not surprising that the second announcement—the one with the details and the map—produced many more donations than the first, generic announcement. Better instructions often lead to better outcomes, as anyone who has had to struggle with a confusing lease, insurance form, or owner's manual can attest.

Yet what *is* surprising is also something that highlights the power of the kind of well-crafted message that a map to a decision is designed to communicate. Before distributing the two announcements, the researchers sent surveys to students in the targeted dorms. The survey asked the students to identify the people in the dorm who were *most* likely to make a donation and the people in the dorm who were *least* likely to make a donation.

Taking the responses as a proxy for charitableness, the researchers used the term "Saints" to describe the students identified as the most likely to donate, and they used the term "Jerks" to describe the students identified as the least likely to donate. The researchers then checked who actually made a donation. Here's what they found:

- Of the Saints who received the generic announcement (without a map), **8 percent** donated.
- Of the Jerks who received the generic announcement (without a map), 0 percent donated.
- Of the Saints who received the detailed announcement (with a map), 42 percent donated.
- Of the Jerks who received the detailed announcement (with a map), **25 percent** donated.

The key numbers here are the 8 percent and the 25 percent. Sending a detailed announcement to a Jerk was much more effective than sending a generic announcement to a Saint. As the Heath brothers put it, the researchers got the worst people in the dorm to donate simply by crafting a more concrete message. "If you're hungry and need a can of food, you're three times better-off relying on a jerk with a map than on a budding young saint without one."

What this means for writing is that we want to make sure our documents (and even our emails and text messages) are as user-friendly as possible. We want to make things easy on readers. We want to write and edit—as we learned in Chapter 3—with empathy.

Readers are busy. Readers are stressed. Readers don't always have an abundance of time, patience, or attention to spare. So if you want to persuade them to make a certain decision or take a particular step, you need to lay out the path in a clear, compelling way.

You need, in other words, to draw them a good map.

Low-Stakes Practice: Mapmakers

They also constituted a map of an abstract conceptual space, a place where, to paraphrase the statistician John Tukey, you were forced to notice what you otherwise wouldn't see.

—Hannah Fry, "Maps without Places" (2021)

Which two of the three excerpts below best capture the idea that writing is a form of mapmaking?

A. "[Musician and producer Jack Antonoff] is often asked how he manages to be so prolific, and has come to resent the question. ('Some people have hobbies. My hobby is taking a break from music to work on other music.')"

—Andrew Marantz, "Jack Antonoff's Gift for Pop-Music Collaboration" (2022)

B. "To write is to carve a new path through the terrain of the imagination, or to point out new features on a familiar route. To read is to travel through that terrain with the author as a guide—a guide one might not always agree with or trust, but who can at least be counted upon to take one somewhere."

—Rebecca Solnit, *Wanderlust: A History of Walking* (2000)

C. "Readers of *The Metaphysical Club* or Louis Menand's critical essays in *The New Yorker*, where he is a staff writer, will recognize the elegant, even-keeled prose in *The Free World*. He aspires to take readers by the hand and walk them through complex abstractions."

—Marc Tracy, "'The Free World' Explains How Culture Heated Up During the Cold War" (2021)

Answer Key

The excerpts from Rebecca Solnit (B) and Marc Tracy (C) best capture the idea that writing is a form of mapmaking. Solnit uses the language of "terrain" and being a good "guide," as does Tracy, if a bit more indirectly. He says that Louis Menand, the author of the book Tracy is reviewing, "aspires to take readers by the hand and walk them through complex abstractions."

As far as the excerpt about Jack Antonoff (A), that one better aligns with the themes of Chapter 2 ("Editing and Interleaving").

High-Stakes Project: Reverse Outline

You may understand the point of your paragraph and why it belongs where it is, but do you make this clear to your reader? Are you giving clear signals about where you're heading? Does your voice work as a thread, running through your paper, guiding and making connections for the reader?

—Amherst College Writing Center, "Reverse Outlining" (2021)

Background

This chapter has focused on the relationship between writing and mapping. With that relationship in mind, take a shot at mapping the structure of your high-stakes project.

A common approach is to create an outline of your project early on in the writing process, before you start your first draft. Feel free to do that. Some people really benefit from taking the time to lay out a detailed overview of the path they intend to forge.

Right now, however, I want you to consider taking a different (or at least additional) approach: also create an outline *after* you finish your first draft.

The term for this post-draft outline is a "reverse outline." Here's how the Amherst College Writing Center explains the benefits: "Reverse outlining helps you to achieve a greater level of objectivity by pulling out the main ideas of your paper, i.e. what you actually said in your draft. If done correctly, it produces a condensed version of your argument that you can evaluate without getting bogged down by style."

The key part of that description is the focus on "what you actually said in your draft." A pre-draft outline is merely speculative. It sets out the map you *hope* to draw for readers. A post-draft outline, on the other hand, is more empirical. It sets out the map you actually drew.

Once you have that bit of cartographic data, you'll have a clearer sense of both the territory you've already covered and the territory you still need to fill in.

Assignment

Take a shot at a reverse outline. If your high-stakes project isn't far enough along for this kind of treatment, pick a document for which you've recently completed at least one draft. It could be a memo for work. It could be a paper for school. It could be an important email or networking note.

The point is to take a fresh look at something you've written and push yourself to identify its major themes, contours, and takeaways. I have my law students do reverse outlines all the time. The exercise is a great way to get a macro-level view of whether you've made good on what you set out to accomplish.

Note: If you are looking for ideas on how to structure your outline, perhaps you'll get some inspiration from a few handwritten ones by famous authors. Photocopies of them are available at the web addresses below.

Joseph Heller's outline of *Catch-22*
- https://biblioklept.org/2013/05/15/joseph-hellers -handwritten-outline-for-catch-22/

Sylvia Plath's outline of *The Bell Jar*
- https://www.bl.uk/collection-items/manuscript-outline -of-chapters-for-the-bell-jar-by-sylvia-plath

Gay Talese's outline of "Frank Sinatra Has a Cold"
- https://theparisreview.tumblr.com/post/43512406636/ gay-taleses-outline-for-frank-sinatra-has-a

A more complete list has been compiled in a post by Emily Temple called "Famous Authors' Handwritten Outlines of Great Works of Literature." As of the publication of this book in the fall of 2022, you could find it on the website Flavorwire: https://www.flavorwire .com/391173/famous-authors-handwritten-outlines-for-great-works -of-literature.

CHAPTER 6

Spotting Sentences

*Sentences come in three forms, which
it is a great convenience to recognize;
for as in all technical definitions, the
knowledge permits the workman to spot
and repair trouble quickly and efficiently.*

—Jacques Barzun, *Simple and Direct:
A Rhetoric for Writers* (1975)

This chapter introduces some foundational editing vocabulary using one of the most gifted writers to ever serve on the US Supreme Court: Justice Oliver Wendell Holmes Jr.

1841–1935

If you can learn to spot the difference among three types of sentences in Holmes's writing—simple, compound, and complex—you'll be well equipped to enhance how you craft some of your own sentences. And don't worry if the labels "simple," "compound," and "complex" are unfamiliar to you. You'll gain a better understanding of them as you work your way through the exercises in this chapter, each of which is designed to be more instructional than evaluative.

Low-Stakes Practice: Help from Holmes

1. A simple sentence consists of one _____.
   —*Merriam-Webster's Manual for Writers & Editors* (1998)

   A. relative pronoun
   B. comma splice
   C. main or independent clause
   D. subordinate or dependent clause

2. Which of these samples from the writings of Justice Holmes is *not* a simple sentence?

   A. "A page of history is worth a volume of logic."
   —*New York Trust Co. v. Eisner* (1921)
   B. "The most stringent protection of free speech would not protect a man in falsely shouting fire in a theatre and causing a panic."
   —*Schenck v. United States* (1919)
   C. "The 14th Amendment does not enact Mr. Herbert Spencer's *Social Statics*."
   —*Lochner v. New York* (1905) (dissenting)
   D. None of the above.

3. A compound sentence consists of _____.
   —*Merriam-Webster's Manual for Writers & Editors* (1998)

   A. two or more main clauses
   B. one main clause and a subordinate clause
   C. a main clause and a dangling modifier
   D. a subordinate clause and a dangling modifier

4. Which of these samples from the writings of Justice Holmes is a compound sentence?

A. "Even a dog distinguishes between being stumbled over and being kicked."

> —*The Common Law* (1881)

B. "But as precedents survive like the clavicle in the cat, long after the use they once served is at an end, and the reason for them has been forgotten, the result of following them must often be failure and confusion from the merely logical point of view."

> —"Common Carriers and the Common Law" (1879)

C. "The law embodies the story of a nation's development through many centuries, and it cannot be dealt with as if it contained only the axioms and corollaries of a book of mathematics."

> —*The Common Law* (1881)

D. "If you want to know the law and nothing else, you must look at it as a bad man, who cares only for the material consequences which such knowledge enables him to predict, not as a good one, who finds his reasons for conduct, whether inside the law or outside of it, in the vaguer sanctions of conscience."

> —"The Path of the Law" (1897)

5. A complex sentence consists of _____.

> —*Merriam-Webster's Manual for Writers & Editors* (1998)

A. three or more main clauses
B. a main clause and one or more subordinate clauses
C. two subordinate clauses
D. a coordinating conjunction and a dash

6. Which of these samples from the writings of Justice Holmes is a complex sentence?

A. "While that experiment is part of our system, I think that we should be eternally vigilant against attempts to check the expression of opinions that we loathe and believe to be fraught with death, unless they so imminently threaten immediate interference with the lawful and pressing purposes of the law that an immediate check is required to save the country."

—*Abrams v. United States* (1919)

B. "Three generations of imbeciles are enough."

—*Buck v. Bell* (1927)

C. "Our test of truth is a reference to either a present or an imagined future majority in favor of our view."

—"Natural Law" (1918)

D. A + C.

7. Based on the questions you have answered so far, try to compose a definition of a "compound-complex" sentence. (Bonus points if your sentence somehow references Justice Holmes.)

Answer Key

1. **C. Main or independent clause:** A simple sentence has one independent clause and nothing else.

2. **D. None of the above:** All the sentences in the answer choices are simple sentences.

3. **A. Two or more main clauses:** A compound sentence consists of two or more independent clauses.

4. **C. "The law embodies the story of a nation's development through many centuries, and it cannot be dealt with as if it contained only the axioms and corollaries of a book of mathematics":** This sentence is a compound sentence. There are two independent clauses and no subordinate clauses (sometimes called "dependent clauses").

5. **B. A main clause and one or more subordinate clauses:** The term *Merriam-Webster* uses for "independent clause" is "main clause," but the definition is essentially the same: a complex sentence consists of a clause that could stand alone as a sentence and at least one clause that can't.

6. **A. "While that experiment is part of our system, I think that we should be eternally vigilant against attempts to check the expression of opinions that we loathe and believe to be fraught with death, unless they so imminently threaten immediate interference with the lawful and pressing purposes of the law that an immediate check is required to save the country":** A complex sentence is a sentence that has an independent clause and at least one subordinate clause. The independent clause in this sentence from Holmes's judicial opinion in *Abrams* is the following: "I think that we should be eternally vigilant against attempts to check the expression of opinions that we loathe and believe to be fraught with death." The subordinate

clauses are "While that experiment is part of our system" and "unless they so imminently threaten immediate interference with the lawful and pressing purposes of the law that an immediate check is required to save the country."

7. The passage below contains a compound-complex sentence from *The Great Dissent: How Oliver Wendell Holmes Changed His Mind—and Changed the History of Free Speech in America* by Thomas Healy. I've underlined the relevant sentence:

> The day before, Holmes had circulated a dissenting opinion in a case the Court had heard two weeks earlier. It was an important case testing the government's power to punish the anarchists and agitators who had spoken out against the recent war. And for most members of the Court, it was an easy case. Of course the government could punish such troublemakers. <u>Freedom of speech was not absolute, and if the defendants had intended to disrupt the war, they deserved to be treated as criminals.</u>

Healy's compound-complex sentence brings together the following elements:

- Two independent clauses ("Freedom of speech was not . . .") and ("they deserved to be . . .")
- One subordinate clause ("if the defendants . . .")

You can compare that ratio to the sentence you composed.

High-Stakes Project: Making Sentences

Your job as a writer is making sentences.

Most of your time will be spent making sentences in your head.

In your head.

Did no one ever tell you this?

That is the writer's life.

Never imagine you've left the level of the sentence behind.

　　　—Verlyn Klinkenborg, *Several Short Sentences about Writing* (2012)

Background

Think of an important document you have recently written. Estimate its percentage of simple sentences, compound sentences, complex sentences, and compound-complex sentences. Write down your estimate on a piece of paper.

Assignment

Now read the document and calculate its actual percentages. How many of the total sentences are simple sentences? Thirty percent? Sixty percent? Ninety percent? How about compound sentences? Complex sentences? Compound-complex? (If the document is long, stick to just the first three pages.)

Once you've figured out the overall breakdown, record those percentages next to your original estimates.

	Estimate	Actual
Simple	_____%	_____%
Compound	_____%	_____%
Complex	_____%	_____%
Compound-Complex	_____%	_____%

- How do you feel about your percentages?
- How do they match up with the percentages you think your intended audience will want?

- How do they match up with the percentages you think a writer who is slightly better than you would have?
- How do they match up with the percentages you think a writer who is a lot better than you would have?
- What steps are you going to take to close these gaps?

For examples of the sentence breakdown of a writer who is slightly better than you, check out the work of someone you admire in your class, organization, or field. For examples of the sentence breakdown of a writer who is a lot better than you, check out the work of someone who has won the Pulitzer Prize, the Man Booker Prize, or even the Nobel Prize. Seeing how these skilled wordsmiths intersperse simple, compound, complex, and even compound-complex sentences will give you a sense of how you might achieve a similar dynamic, engaging balance. When trying to improve, it is often helpful to have a clear target.

* * * *

Past winners of the Pulitzer Prize can be found at https://www .pulitzer.org/prize-winners-by-year.

Past winners of the Man Booker Prize can be found at https:// thebookerprizes.com/.

Past winners of the Nobel Prize (in Literature) can be found at https://www.nobelprize.org/prizes/lists/all-nobel-prizes-in -literature/.

PART IV

What it meant to be a writer—imaginatively and morally—had interested Joan Didion since she spent her teen-age years retyping Hemingway's sentences, trying to understand the way they worked.

—Nathan Heller, "The Falconer" (2021)

PREVIOUSLY ON

This version of Previously On draws on more than just concepts from the most recent chapters:

- "Writing as Mapping" (Chapter 5)
- "Spotting Sentences" (Chapter 6)

It also tests your recall of concepts from earlier chapters.

- "Editing and Empathy" (Chapter 1)
- "Editing and Interleaving" (Chapter 2)
- "Anticipatory Edits" (Chapter 3)
- "The Animal Farm Principle" (Chapter 4)

Regularly trying to retrieve information is an important part of learning, especially when significant time has passed since you first encountered the information.

* * *

Identify the chapter where each passage appeared.

1. "We rush to cram as much information as possible into our arguments and explanations, forgetting that an overstuffed brief, memo, or report is not at all user-friendly. Judges and other key decision-makers already have many other overstuffed things in their lives: calendars, desks, briefcases, email inboxes. Why tax their brains (and their time) even

more? Why not instead begin by thinking about what kind of document you would like to read if you were in their position?"

A. "Spotting Sentences"
B. "Editing and Empathy"
C. "Anticipatory Edits"
D. "Editing and Interleaving"

2. "Sentences come in three forms, which it is a great convenience to recognize; for as in all technical definitions, the knowledge permits the workman to spot and repair trouble quickly and efficiently."

A. "Editing and Empathy"
B. "Editing and Interleaving"
C. "The Animal Farm Principle"
D. "Spotting Sentences"

3. "The term for this post-draft outline is a 'reverse outline.' Here's how the Writing Center at Amherst College explains the benefits: 'Reverse outlining helps you to achieve a greater level of objectivity by pulling out the main ideas of your paper, i.e. what you actually said in your draft. If done correctly, it produces a condensed version of your argument that you can evaluate without getting bogged down by style.'"

A. "Editing and Empathy"
B. "Editing and Interleaving"
C. "The Animal Farm Principle"
D. "Writing as Mapping"

Answer Key

1. **B. "Editing and Empathy"**: The passage appeared in the "Editing and Empathy" chapter. The sentence right after the ones included in the passage mentions "empathy" specifically: "Why tax their brains (and their time) even more? Why not instead begin by thinking about what kind of document you would like to read if you were in their position? Why not start with empathy?"

2. **D. "Spotting Sentences"**: The sentence appeared as an epigraph to the "Spotting Sentences" chapter. It comes from the book *Simple and Direct: A Rhetoric for Writers* by Jacques Barzun, who taught history for many decades at Columbia University and received a number of honors, including the Presidential Medal of Freedom from George W. Bush, the National Humanities Medal from Barack Obama, and knighthood in the French Legion of Honor. "Simple English is no one's mother tongue," Barzun once remarked. "It has to be worked for." One of his final books, *From Dawn to Decadence*, was nominated for the National Book Critics Award in 2000. Barzun was 92 years old when he published it, and he continued to write until his death at the age of 104.

3. **D. "Writing as Mapping"**: The idea of a "reverse outline" was introduced in the High-Stakes Project section of the "Writing as Mapping" chapter. That section also included the following epigraph from the Amherst College Writing Center:

> You may understand the point of your paragraph and why it belongs where it is, but do you make

this clear to your reader? Are you giving clear signals about where you're heading? Does your voice work as a thread, running through your paper, guiding and making connections for the reader?

CHAPTER 7

Shot Selection

The simple declarative sentence used in making a plain statement is one sound. But Lord love ye it mustn't be worked to death.

—Robert Frost, Letter to John Bartlett (July 4, 1913)

One of the more common pieces of writing advice in our post-Hemingway world is to keep sentences short. Experts on legal writing are particularly fond of this position—and for good reason. When judges read the sentences that appear in the briefs, memos, statutes, and contracts that come across their desks, I doubt many of them say, "You know what each of these sentences could use? More words."

In *The Art of Advocacy*, Noah Messing of Yale Law School does an especially good job making the case for short sentences. Brevity, he explains, "reduces the risk that your writing will confuse or irk readers," especially given that "empirical studies show that writing verbosely makes writers sound *dumber*, not smarter." He even suggests that struggling writers consider self-imposing a strict twenty-five-word limit. He admits that the limit will sound radical to some people, but he insists that it produces remarkable results. "Simply by keeping sentences under twenty-five words, writers ensure that they comply with many of the principles of good style. They hack wordy phrases, cut passive verbs, and limit the number of ideas in any given sentence, among other salutary changes. The results tend to thrill clients and supervisors, both because coping with the twenty-five-word limit causes writing to sparkle and because short sentences are *vastly* easier for them to edit."

Yet Messing and others caution against taking a commitment to concision too far. "Even as you follow my advice to write short sentences," he warns, "beware of one grave risk. If every sentence resembles every other sentence, your prose will grow dull, sound robotic, or convey anger." None of those qualities scream "skillful writer."

The standard remedy for this off-putting homogeneity is to vary your sentence structure, a practice I have persuaded my students to adopt by encouraging them to consider the importance of "shot selection." Think of a basketball team, I tell them. To be successful, the players must be able to make long shots, like three-pointers, and they must also be able to make short shots, like lay-ups and dunks. A team that relies on only one form of scoring will become predictable, even boring. Variety makes them more effective. And more fun to watch.

The same is true in tennis. A tennis player who only excels back on the baseline or up at the net will not go as far as a tennis player who excels both back on the baseline *and* up at the net. Nor will someone who only has a  good forehand go as far as someone who has both a good forehand and a good backhand.

Part of why many people consider Roger Federer the greatest tennis player of all time is the completeness of his skill set. As the writer David Foster Wallace explained in 2006, the range of Federer's game inspires a profound sense of awe:

> Federer's forehand is a great liquid whip, his backhand a one-hander that can drive flat, load with topspin, or slice—the slice with such snap that the ball turns shapes in the air and skids on the grass to maybe ankle height. His serve has world-class pace and a degree of placement and variety no one else comes close to; the service motion is lithe and uneccentric, distinctive (on TV) only in a certain eel-like all-body snap at the moment of impact. His anticipation and court sense are otherworldly, and his footwork is the best in the game—as a child, he was also a soccer prodigy.

Imagine if your writing had Federer's grace and versatility. Imagine if you could communicate in more than one mode, at more than one velocity, and through more than one syntactic configuration. Think of the range of thoughts you'd be able to articulate and how nimble and customized you could make your arguments. One-dimensional writing is not very persuasive. The best advocates have a much bigger repertoire of shots.

A. Vital and Alive

When I say "repertoire of shots," I mean to include more than just a range of sentence structures. I also mean to include a range of sentence lengths. Which is why I often ask my law students to try the following exercise:

1. Circle the longest sentence on a page of your writing.
2. Then circle the shortest sentence.
3. Now subtract the length of the shortest sentence from the length of the longest sentence.

If your longest sentence is thirty-six words and your shortest sentence is thirty-four words, you have a problem. If your longest sentence is eight words and your shortest sentence is six words, you also have a problem. In fact, even if your longest sentence is twenty-one words and your shortest sentence is nineteen words—making your average sentence length right around that sweet spot of twenty words recommended by many style guides—you still have a problem. The range of your sentences, in all these cases, is way too uniform.

Joseph Williams, who taught for many years at the University of Chicago, captures the issue nicely in *Style: Toward Clarity and Grace*. He doesn't use an analogy to basketball or tennis. Instead, he uses an analogy to music. "If you never write sentences longer than twenty words, you'll be like a pianist who uses only the middle octave; you can carry the tune, but without much variety or range."

The travel writer and novelist Pico Iyer takes a similar position. Short sentences, he says, are "the domain of uninflected talk-radio rants and shouting heads on TV who feel that qualification or sub-tlety is an assault on their integrity (and not, as it truly is, integrity's greatest adornment)." He even worries that "if we continue along this road, whole areas of feeling and cognition and experience will be lost to us." Brevity is efficient, he acknowledges, but at what cost?

Iyer suggests we use longer sentences—which are more hospita-ble to depth and nuance—as a way to resist the speed and urgency of texts, news flashes, and constantly updating internet feeds. "Not everyone," he says, "wants to be reduced to a sound bite or a bumper sticker."

Even Dr. Seuss advocated for more variety in sentence length. "Simple, short sentences don't always do the work," he advised in a 1965 issue of the *Saturday Evening Post*. "You have to do tricks with pacing, alternate long sentences with short, to keep [your writing] vital and alive."

B. Catch Their Breath

The appeal of the long-short alternation that Dr. Seuss describes has another champion: the award-winning journalist Meghan Daum. "I use a lot of short sentences—I like staccato," she told Ben Yagoda during an interview for Yagoda's 2004 book *The Sound on the Page*. "After a long riff, I always have a short one after it, for readers to catch their breath."

Daum's reader-focused sensibility is a great way to begin to develop your own mix of long and short sentences. Have you recently made your readers navigate some tricky syntax and absorb a lot of complex information? Do you think they might now appreciate a quick cognitive break to reset and recover? If they were up on a stage performing your words as a monologue, would they need to take a deep breath before continuing?

If so, perhaps it is time to treat them to a shorter, simpler sentence. You don't want to overly tax their brains or their patience. Three-point shots are difficult to pull off, especially several times in a row. Sometimes the better choice is a lay-up.

To see what I mean, we'll stick with the basketball theme and look at an excerpt from a book about the 1979–80 Portland Trail Blazers by the Pulitzer Prize–winning journalist David Halberstam. Notice how Halberstam strategically places three short sentences to balance the rhythm and overall mental load of the passage.

> For the first time, Greg Bunch was willing to say a few guarded words to Abdul Jeelani, a very few words indeed. They did not go out to eat together; there was too much tension in the air for that. Jeelani preferred in any case to eat out with Steve Hayes, whom he had known and played against in Italy. But he worried about Bunch, who was so tight that he could not sleep at night, always tossing and turning in bed. Jeelani in one sense wanted to befriend Greg Bunch, but he was aware, in the most primitive way possible, that everything good which happened to Bunch was bad for Abdul Jeelani. <u>It was terrible to think that way</u>. <u>So he kept his distance from Bunch</u>. At the same time he couldn't help realizing that the fear and tension in the face of his roommate was the same fear and tension he had seen on his own face during his three previous NBA tryouts, in Detroit, in Cleveland, in New Orleans, when he had looked around him and become convinced that everyone there, rookies, veterans, coaches, scouts, wanted him to fail. <u>At this camp Jeelani felt more confident, more mature</u>. He had three years of European ball behind him and he knew that only one player—Jimmy Paxson, a guard and thus not a competitor—had guaranteed money.

C. "I Am an Invisible Man"

Another good place for a short sentence is at the beginning of a paragraph, especially if that paragraph contains a number of more syntactically sophisticated sentences. Here, for example, is how Ralph

Ellison opens *Invisible Man*, the novel that beat out Ernest Heming-way's *The Old Man and the Sea* for the National Book Award in 1953 and has since become one of the most celebrated works of fiction in American literature.

> I am an invisible man. No, I am not a spook like those who haunted Edgar Allan Poe; nor am I one of your Hollywood-movie ectoplasms.  I am a man of substance, of flesh and bone, fiber and liquids—and I might even be said to possess a mind. I am invisible, under-stand, simply because people refuse to see me. Like the bodiless heads you see some-times in circus sideshows, it is as though I have been surrounded by mirrors of hard, distorting glass. When they approach me they see only my surroundings, themselves, or figments of their imagination—indeed, everything and anything except me.

Notice the contrast between the short, punchy first sentence—"I am an invisible man"—and the longer, more layered sentences that follow it. There's a virtuosic boldness to that kind of beginning. Ellison starts incredibly fast, leading with a statement that is as forceful as it is brief. But then he gradually expands his thoughts through an elongated, almost jazzlike set of rhythms, caveats, and meditations.

Below are two more examples. Neither quite matches the musi-cality of Ellison, who played the trumpet for many years and initially planned to be a classical composer. But both do, in their own way, present a compelling mix of concision and complexity.

The first example comes from the opening paragraph of Herman Melville's 1851 classic *Moby Dick*. The second appears in the open-ing paragraph of a more commercially popular book, *The Martian* by Andy Weir, which was adapted into a Hollywood movie starring Matt Damon in 2015. To help highlight the admirable sentence range

Melville and Weir employ, I've underlined not just the short sentences that begin the paragraphs but also the longest sentences nearby.

Herman Melville, *Moby Dick* (1851)

<u>Call me Ishmael.</u> Some years ago—never mind how long precisely—having little or no money in my purse, and nothing particular to interest me on shore, I thought I would sail about a little and see the watery part of the world. It is a way I have of driving off the spleen, and regulating the circulation. <u>Whenever I find myself growing grim about the mouth; whenever it is a damp, drizzly November in my soul; whenever I find myself involuntarily pausing before coffin warehouses, and bringing up the rear of every funeral I meet; and especially whenever my hypos get such an upper hand of me, that it requires a strong moral principle to prevent me from deliberately stepping into the street, and methodically knocking people's hats off—then, I account it high time to get to sea as soon as I can.</u>

Andy Weir, *The Martian* (2011)

<u>I'm pretty much fucked.</u>
    That's my considered opinion.
    Fucked.
    Six days into what should be the greatest month of my life, and it's turned into a nightmare.
    I don't even know who'll read this. I guess someone will find it eventually. Maybe a hundred years from now.
    For the record . . . I didn't die on Sol 6. Certainly the rest of the crew thought I did, and I can't blame them. <u>Maybe there'll be a day of national mourning for me, and my Wikipedia page will say, "Mark Watney is the only human being to have died on Mars."</u>

Just like Ellison does, Melville and Weir each start their stories with a sentence that is simple, direct, and inviting. They reduce the reader's barrier to entry. They lay out a kind of grammatical welcome mat. "Come in," they seem to be saying. "Don't be intimidated. There may be complex material in here, but I promise to be your guide."

D. Blackmon Bow

A third place to consider the interplay of short and long sentences is at the end of a paragraph. Few things cap big thoughts better than a tidy, summative closing. After being introduced to an idea and seeing it develop, there can be something wonderful about receiving it in a more compact, clarifying form. Short sentences have a nice way of doing that. They're sort of like elegant little bows you attach to finalize and enhance a structured package of content.

I first started showing students this bow technique using excerpts from *Slavery by Another Name: The Re-enslavement of Black Americans from the Civil War to World War II* by Douglas Blackmon. I was teaching a course called "The Syntax of Slavery," and Blackmon's book provided both a helpful account of an often-overlooked part of American history and a superb model of effective storytelling. Here is how the first chapter opens. Note the snappy "bow" at the end of the second paragraph:

> On March 30, 1908, Green Cottenham was arrested by the sheriff of Shelby County, Alabama, and charged with "vagrancy." Cottenham had committed no true crime. Vagrancy, the offense of a person not being able to prove at a given moment that he or she is employed, was a new and flimsy concoction dredged up from legal obscurity at the end of the nineteenth century by the state legislatures of Alabama and other southern states. It was capriciously enforced by local sheriffs and constables, adjudicated by mayors and notaries public, recorded haphazardly or not at all in court records, and, most tellingly in a time of massive unemployment among all southern men, was reserved almost exclusively for black men. Cottenham's offense was blackness.

My students and I started referring to this move as the "Blackmon Bow." It's not a great name, but it worked for us, and I soon noticed an uptick in the number of their paragraphs that closed with a punch.

When I have explained the move to other groups of people, some preferred to call it a "bow tie," a term that adds an extra bit of class to the construction. Either name works. So does no name at all. The point is simply to be more deliberate about how you end paragraphs and also to notice when something pithy may be the way to go. Good advocates close with confidence.

E. "Not So"

There's one more situation in which pairing short and long sentences seems especially valuable: when you want to refute an argument.

One of my office neighbors at the University of Michigan Law School, the bankruptcy expert Professor John Pottow, used this technique quite well in *Executive Benefits Insurance Agency v. Arkinson*, an important US Supreme Court case he argued (and won!) in 2014. He first identifies the position that the opposite side, Executive Benefits Insurance Agency (or "EBIA"), was trying to advance: "EBIA attempts to distinguish *Roell* by arguing that it was decided on statutory grounds alone and thus has no relevance to Article III issues." Next, he immediately dismisses that position with a short, sharp retort: "But EBIA's reading is too wooden."

It's not the fanciest of rhetorical moves, but it is an effective one. With six crisp words, Professor Pottow flattens EBIA's interpretation of a key bit of precedent and begins to prepare the justices to adopt a different approach.

Some lawyers pull off this kind of maneuver even more concisely. One of them is Tom Goldstein, the founder of the Peabody Award–winning website SCOTUSblog. While representing a high-profile client charged with operating an illegal sports gambling ring in Las Vegas, he used just two words—"Not so"—to counter one of the prosecutor's main arguments. Nothing more was needed.

As powerful as Goldstein's compositional frugality was, however, there's certainly a danger in employing it too often, like a trick shot that becomes mundane, even obnoxious, the more times you see it. But the general technique of having a short sentence refute the other side's stated position remains sound. Short sentences communicate confidence. They don't hem. They don't haw. They don't get lost in equivocations and caveats.  They get right to the point, sometimes devastatingly—which can be a good thing when you are taking on a mistaken point of view. "Pithy sentences," the Enlightenment philosopher Denis Diderot observes, "are like sharp nails that force truth upon our memory." Used in the right places, they pack a persuasive punch.

Low-Stakes Practice: Pleasing Cadence

It's kind of like when you read a good author, and they mix short and long sentences. I loved the way it fluctuated your expectations.

—Television writer and producer Robert King describing the varied pacing of *The Sopranos*, *Mad Men*, and other well-crafted shows

Below are a few endorsements of the "shot selection" approach to sentence construction that we just covered. Under each is a doctored passage by the author of the endorsement. I say "doctored" because I have removed the periods. Your job is to put them back. Doing so will force you to think about the length of the sentences the authors wanted to create. It will also help you internalize the rhythm that goes into these kinds of judgment calls.

Because leaving in the capital letters would clue you in to where the periods go, I have changed all but the first word in each passage to lowercase. You'll need to decide which ones would switch back to having capital letters. You'll also, for question two, need to insert some paragraph breaks.

1. **Author:** Teju Cole (Gore Vidal Professor of the Practice of Creative Writing at Harvard University)

   Endorsement: "Vary . . . the rhythm of your sentences. Most of them should be short, but the occasional long one will give a musical and pleasing cadence to your writing."

   Passage (without periods): "My second suggestion is that you remove all clichés from your writing—spare not a single one—the cliché is an element of herd thinking, and writers should be solitary animals phrases that have been used to the point of becoming meaningless have no place in your stories 'money doesn't grow on trees,' 'not my cup of tea,' 'everything happens for a reason': mildewed language of this kind is a waste of the reader's time."

2. **Author:** Ross Guberman (President of Legal Writing Pro)

   Endorsement: "Everyone complains that lawyers' sentences are too long. But I wish critics were as passionate about including short sentences. What makes prose sing, after all, is variety in sentence length and structure, not adhering to strict medium-sentence-only rules.

   Let me propose a different goal, one that is also more fun to strive for: on each page of your brief, include at least one sentence that starts and stops on the same line of text."

   Passage (without periods): "When I work with attorneys in law firms, I often ask the associates if they think the partners' final drafts are better than their own they generally do if I ask them why, I nearly always hear the word *punchy* in response the associates may be on to something: As a group, senior partners write 'punchier' motions and briefs than junior lawyers do and the most renowned advocates of all write 'punchier' motions and briefs than most of those senior partners do one reason is that experience begets confidence, confidence begets joy, and joy begets fresh, conversational language."

3. **Author:** Noah Lukeman (Literary Agent)

   Endorsement: "Remember: writing is about *contrast*. If all sentences are short, the effect is lost. Nothing stands out. But if many sentences are long (or at least of medium length), and then a short sentence comes along, that sentence will have the desired effect. This is also one of the ways to add meaning to a sentence without hitting the reader over the head; the brevity will resonate with the reader in a more subtle, refined way."

   Passage (without periods): "Punctuation is the music of language as a conductor can influence the experience of the song by manipulating its rhythm, so can punctuation influence the reading experience, bring out the best (or worst) in a text by controlling the speed of a text, punctuation dictates how it should be read a delicate world of punctuation lives just beneath the surface of your work, like a world of microorganisms living in a pond they are missed by the naked eye, but if you use a microscope you will find it exists, and that the pond is, in fact, teeming with life."

Answer Key

1. **Author:** Teju Cole

   Passage: "My second suggestion is that you remove all clichés from your writing. Spare not a single one. The cliché is an element of herd thinking, and writers should be solitary animals. Phrases that have been used to the point of becoming meaningless have no place in your stories. 'Money doesn't grow on trees,' 'Not my cup of tea,' 'Everything happens for a reason': mildewed language of this kind is a waste of the reader's time."

2. **Author:** Ross Guberman

   Passage: "When I work with attorneys in law firms, I often ask the associates if they think the partners' final drafts are better than their own. They generally do. If I ask them why, I nearly always hear the word *punchy* in response.

   The associates may be on to something: As a group, senior partners write 'punchier' motions and briefs than junior lawyers do. And the most renowned advocates of all write 'punchier' motions and briefs than most of those senior partners do.

   One reason is that experience begets confidence, confidence begets joy, and joy begets fresh, conversational language."

3. **Author:** Noah Lukeman

   Passage: "Punctuation is the music of language. As a conductor can influence the experience of the song by manipulating its rhythm, so can punctuation influence the reading experience, bring out the best (or worst) in a text. By controlling the speed of a text, punctuation dictates how it should be read. A delicate world of punctuation lives just beneath the surface of your work, like a world of microorganisms living in a pond. They are missed by the naked eye, but if you use a microscope you will find it exists, and that the pond is, in fact, teeming with life."

High-Stakes Project: Range Rover

An assumption exists that long sentences are bad, but it is usually the case that bad sentences are long.

—Brooks Landon, *Building Great Sentences* (2008)

Background

The nice thing about the concept of "shot selection" is that you can pretty easily get some data on how well your own sentences implement it. Simply count the number of words in them—or at least in a representative sample.

Assignment

Step 1: Take a look at your high-stakes project.

Step 2: If your project is shorter than or equal to three pages in length, go through the whole thing. If it's longer than that, pick up to three pages to target.

Step 3: Find your longest sentence on each page. Count the number of words.

Step 4: Find the shortest sentence on each page. Count the number of words.

Step 5: Calculate your sentence range: the difference between the number of words in your longest sentence and the number of words in your shortest sentence.

Step 6: Compare your sentence range to the sentence range of one of your favorite authors or publications. How does yours match up?

You might also pick something created by a coworker or fellow student whose writing you admire. The point is to see where you stand in relation to a desirable benchmark. If there is a big gap—if your sentence range is four words and the benchmark is thirty-five words—adjust accordingly.

CHAPTER 8

Paragraphing

There is a style of paragraphing as well as a style of sentence structure.

—Edward P. J. Corbett, *Classical Rhetoric for the Modern Student* (1971)

Consider treating the word "paragraph" as a verb. Think of it as something you can do well or poorly, with major consequences for your readers.

Good paragraphers, for example, help readers. They make information easy to navigate and absorb. They don't flit around, hastily moving on to the next point before fully supporting their first. Nor do they get stuck for too long in one place. Instead, they give a lot of thought not just to the ideas they generate but also to the arrangement of those ideas—their shape, their balance, their pace.

Bad paragraphers aren't nearly as considerate. They don't think much at all, or at least not about the way they communicate and position their content. They're perfectly fine burdening people's brains with pages and pages of undifferentiated text.

Just as irritatingly, they too often toss in one-sentence paragraphs. When used sparingly, one-sentence paragraphs can produce a powerfully effective contrast, particularly if the sentence contains a statement that is bold and bracing. But when used indiscriminately, they become a distracting habit. As the journalist Andy Bodle has pointed out, the wonderful one-sentence paragraph that closes F. Scott Fitzgerald's classic novel *The Great Gatsby*—"So we beat on, boats against the current, borne back ceaselessly into the past"—would lose much of its force if every preceding paragraph were also that length. "Lots of short paragraphs," he explains, "create the impression of a series of unconnected slogans." Prose with punch is good. Prose without progression is not. Good writing has more to offer than just soundbites.

A. Pinker's Pointers

In *The Sense of Style: The Thinking Person's Guide to Writing in the 21st Century*, the Harvard psychologist Steven Pinker offers a way to assess the two extremes of bad paragraphing. He first focuses on those instances that need more breaks. "Sometimes a writer should cleave an intimidating block of print with a paragraph break to give the reader's eyes a place to alight and rest," he suggests. He adds that academic writers "often neglect to do this and trowel out massive slabs of visually monotonous text."

He then addresses the opposite concern: "Newspaper journalists, mindful of their readers' attention spans, sometimes go to the other extreme and dice their text into nanographs consisting of a sentence or two apiece."

In Pinker's view, inexperienced writers more often adopt the over-packed approach of academics than the underpacked approach of journalists. They don't use enough paragraphs and could benefit tremendously by thinking more strategically about including visual breaks. "It's always good to show mercy to your readers and periodically let them rest their weary eyes," he advises. "Just be sure not to derail them in the middle of a train of thought."

B. Everything Went Wrong

The Low-Stakes Practice section of this chapter contains a paragraphing-focused exercise I do with my law students. I give them a big chunk of unparagraphed text and ask them to read it over. I then tell them to identify where they think the paragraph breaks should go, as if they were composing the piece of writing themselves.

Among my favorite samples to use is a legal brief written by Paul Reingold, who taught at the University of Michigan Law School for over thirty-five years before retiring in 2019. The brief is one in which Reingold teamed up with former Michigan Supreme Court justice Charles Levin to represent Matthew Makowski, a forty-five-year-old man who had been sentenced to life without parole back when he was twenty for his part in a robbery that, although intended to be without weapons, ended up leading to the death of one of Makowski's coworkers. Here's the opening part of the "Statement of Facts" section. See if you can find where Reingold and Levin put their paragraph break:

The Crime: The facts of the crime are not in dispute. In 1988 Mr. Makowski was 20 years old. He had no criminal history. He worked as a manager at a Dearborn health club. He had two young employees who, like him, were also bodybuilders and athletes. Mr. Makowski gave cash from the club to one of the employees and sent him out to get a money order. Mr. Makowski conspired with the second employee and that employee's roommate (whom the first employee did not know by sight) to intercept the courier and steal the money. Mr. Makowski said he would share the proceeds with the second worker and his roommate-robber. Everything went wrong. What was supposed to be an unarmed robbery became a murder committed during a robbery when the courier got the better of the roommate-robber and threw him down. The robber pulled a small folding jack-knife, stabbed the courier twice, and fled with the cash ($300 of which went to Mr. Makowski). The courier—Pete Puma—died later that night at the hospital.

The paragraph break chosen by Reingold and Levin—who represented Makowski pro bono—goes right before "Everything went wrong," a sentence I absolutely love. Here's the visual again. Notice how the spacing signals to the reader that we are moving on to a new thought and a new scene:

The Crime: The facts of the crime are not in dispute. In 1988 Mr. Makowski was 20 years old. He had no criminal history. He worked as a manager at a Dearborn health club. He had two young employees who, like him, were also bodybuilders and athletes. Mr. Makowski gave cash from the club to one of the employees and sent him out to get a money order. Mr. Makowski conspired with the second employee and that employee's roommate (whom the first employee did not know by sight) to intercept the courier and steal the money. Mr. Makowski said he would share the proceeds with the second worker and his roommate-robber.

Everything went wrong. What was supposed to be an unarmed robbery became a murder committed during a robbery when the courier got the better of the roommate-robber and threw him down. The robber pulled a small folding jackknife, stabbed the courier twice, and fled with the cash ($300 of which went to Mr. Makowski). The courier—Pete Puma—died later that night at the hospital.

Paragraph breaks are great at providing that kind of guidance. They're stage directions for your brain.

They're also, in this instance, an act of persuasion. The main issue in the case was whether the Michigan governor at the time, Jennifer Granholm, had the authority to rescind her decision to reduce Makowski's sentence of life without parole to a sentence of life *with* the chance of parole, given that all the following steps of the modification process had already been completed:[*]

- Governor Granholm had signed the letter authorizing the reduced sentence, after having received a recommendation from the parole board to issue it.

- Governor Granholm then sent that letter to the secretary of state's office, where it was signed again, affixed with a gold foil seal, and sent back to the governor for delivery to the Michigan Department of Corrections.

- Governor Granholm had authorized her deputy legal counsel to email the Michigan Department of Corrections announcing the reduced sentence, a message that, according to the deposition

---

[*] The technical term for Granholm's original decision is *commutation*. Here's how *Black's Law Dictionary* defines that process: "The executive's substitution in a particular case of a less severe punishment for a more severe one that has already been judicially imposed on the defendant."

testimony of the deputy legal counsel herself, is considered "the final piece" of the process.

Reingold and Levin relied on an extended analogy to the landmark US Supreme Court case *Marbury v. Madison* to argue that the time to cancel the reduction had now passed. In their view, the required signatures had been applied after careful consideration on a variety of levels, and the appropriate seals had been affixed. The deal was, in effect, done. It would be constitutionally improper to undo the whole process.

But that was just their legal argument. Reingold and Levin also devoted significant space in the brief to the more human aspect of the case. They needed to show that Makowski, as a person, deserved a shot at parole.

C. Model Inmate, Severe Sentence

Part of their plan involved highlighting how Makowski, now white-haired and middle-aged, had been a model inmate for the past twenty-five years. They explained that during his entire time in prison, he had been issued only two misconduct tickets. One infraction was for possessing "contraband," which turned out to be a piece of cheese. The other was for "dissent." Makowski received it for disagreeing with an authority figure while serving as a cellblock representative.

This near-perfect record helped Makowski earn the respect of the prison staff, many of whom personally congratulated him when they learned of the governor's original decision to reduce his sentence. It also boosted his case in front of the parole-board members. They're the ones who originally recommended that the governor lower Makowski's sentence down to something that would someday give him a chance at parole.

Another part of the plan—the part that Reingold and Levin's first bit of great paragraphing advances—was to stress the disconnect between Makowski's small, nonviolent role in the robbery and the severity of his original sentence. Makowski did not commit the murder. Nor did he intend for the robber to even carry a weapon. Having stayed at the health club, he was nowhere near the fatal altercation.

Reingold and Levin's third paragraph highlights those important details. Here it is, combined with the two paragraphs we have already seen, to give you a sense of how all three work together:

> **The Crime:** The facts of the crime are not in dispute. In 1988 Mr. Makowski was 20 years old. He had no criminal history. He worked as a manager at a Dearborn health club. He had two young employees who, like him, were also bodybuilders and athletes. Mr. Makowski gave cash from the club to one of the employees and sent him out to get a money order. Mr. Makowski conspired with the second employee and that employee's roommate (whom the first employee did not know by sight) to intercept the courier and steal the money. Mr. Makowski said he would share the proceeds with the second worker and his roommate-robber.
>
> Everything went wrong. What was supposed to be an unarmed robbery became a murder committed during a robbery when the courier got the better of the roommate-robber and threw him down. The robber pulled a small folding jackknife, stabbed the courier twice, and fled with the cash ($300 of which went to Mr. Makowski). The courier—Pete Puma—died later that night at the hospital.
>
> Mr. Makowski was charged with first degree murder and armed robbery. At trial the second employee testified that, to his knowledge, Mr. Makowski never knew that the roommate-robber had a knife. The robber confirmed that testimony:
>
> > Q. Did you ever tell [Mr. Makowski] that you were carrying a knife?
> >
> > A. No.
> >
> > Q. Did he ever tell you to use that knife?

A. No.

Q. As far as you knew, did Matt Makowski ever know that you had a knife?

A. No, no one knew I had a knife.

The jury nonetheless convicted Makowski of first-degree (felony) murder and armed robbery. He was sentenced to mandatory life in prison under MCL 750.316.11.

All three of these paragraphs have a separate focus and function. All three do different work. But because that work is complementary, a coherent story and argument develop.

That's exactly what you want from paragraphs. You want development. You want progression. You want them to create a natural sense of movement from one idea to the next. Reingold and Levin do that throughout their brief—which may be one reason the Michigan Supreme Court ruled in their favor and blocked Governor Granholm from rescinding Makowski's reduced sentence. Less skilled paragraphers might not have been quite as persuasive.

Low-Stakes Practice: The Rhythms of Roth

In general, I would suggest, the paragraph could be understood as a sort of literary respiration, with each paragraph as an extended—in some cases very extended—breath. Inhale at the beginning of the paragraph, exhale at the end. Inhale again at the start of the next.

—Francine Prose, *Reading Like a Writer* (2006)

Background

Following the death of the American writer Philip Roth in 2018, the *Economist* ran an obituary that celebrated, among other things, the way Roth crafted paragraphs. "His paragraphs are written to careful rhythms," the piece notes, "from incantatory to fulminatory with every step in between."*

That kind of compositional range is difficult to achieve. But an important first step is to recognize where paragraphs should start and stop. Use the excerpts below to help you practice making these kinds of decisions. The first two are taken from Roth's own writing. Your job is to find where he and the other authors listed decided to create their paragraph breaks. I've hidden each person's choices by presenting the excerpts as undifferentiated blobs.

Assignment

1. **Philip Roth (*American Pastoral*):** This excerpt comes from the opening paragraphs of *American Pastoral*, a novel that earned Roth a Pulitzer Prize in 1997.

---

* "Incantatory" is a word that is often used to describe something with magical qualities. "Fulminatory" is a word that is often used to describe something that is angry and thunderous. MERRIAM-WEBSTER DICTIONARY (new ed. 2016). Both, appropriately, seem like words that Roth—whose vocabulary was as sophisticated as his paragraphs were powerful—might use himself.

The Swede. During the war years, when I was still a grade
school boy, this was a magical name in our Newark neighborhood, even to adults just a generation removed from the city's
old Prince Street ghetto and not yet so flawlessly Americanized as to be bowled over by the prowess of a high school
athlete. The name was magical; so was the anomalous face.
Of the few fair-complexioned Jewish students in our preponderantly Jewish public high school, none possessed anything
remotely like the steep-jawed, insentient Viking mask of this
blue-eyed blond born into our tribe as Seymour Irving Levov.
The Swede starred as end in football, center in basketball,
and first baseman in baseball. Only the basketball team was
ever any good—twice winning the city championship while
he was its leading scorer—but as long as the Swede excelled,
the fate of our sports teams didn't matter much to a student
body whose elders, largely undereducated and overburdened,
venerated academic achievement above all else. Physical
aggression, even camouflaged by athletic uniforms and official
rules and intended to do no harm to Jews, was not a traditional
source of pleasure in our community—advanced degrees were.
Nonetheless, through the Swede, the neighborhood entered
into a fantasy about itself and about the world, the fantasy of
sports fans everywhere: almost like Gentiles (as they imagined
Gentiles), our families could forget the way things actually
work and make an athletic performance the repository of all
their hopes. Primarily, they could forget the war. The elevation
of Swede Levov into the household Apollo of the Weequahic
Jews can best be explained, I think, by the war against the
Germans and the Japanese and the fears that it fostered. With
the Swede indomitable on the playing field, the meaningless
surface of life provided a bizarre, delusionary kind of sustenance, the happy release into a Swedian innocence, for those

who lived in dread of never seeing their sons or their brothers
or their husbands again.

2. **Philip Roth (Wikipedia letter):** This next excerpt comes from
an open letter Roth wrote to Wikipedia after unsuccessfully
trying to correct some errors listed in an entry for his best-
selling 2000 novel *The Human Stain.* The book was later turned
into a movie starring Nicole Kidman and Anthony Hopkins.
The letter was published by the *New Yorker*.

> Dear Wikipedia,
>
> I am Philip Roth. I had reason recently to read for the
> first time the Wikipedia entry discussing my novel "The
> Human Stain." The entry contains a serious misstatement
> that I would like to ask to have removed. This item entered
> Wikipedia not from the world of truthfulness but from
> the babble of literary gossip—there is no truth in it at
> all. Yet when, through an official interlocutor, I recently
> petitioned Wikipedia to delete this misstatement, along
> with two others, my interlocutor was told by the "English
> Wikipedia Administrator"—in a letter dated August 25th
> and addressed to my interlocutor—that I, Roth, was not a
> credible source: "I understand your point that the author is
> the greatest authority on their own work," writes the Wiki-
> pedia Administrator—"but we require secondary sources."
> Thus was created the occasion for this open letter. After
> failing to get a change made through the usual channels, I
> don't know how else to proceed.

3. **Justice Sandra Day O'Connor:** In 2003, the Supreme Court
ultimately ruled in *Grutter v. Bollinger* that because the University of Michigan Law School had a compelling interest in

attaining a diverse student body, the admissions office's narrowly tailored policy of giving special consideration to certain underrepresented minority groups did not violate the Equal Protection Clause of the Fourteenth Amendment. Justice Sandra Day O'Connor wrote the majority opinion in what has become one of the court's landmark decisions on affirmative action. Find the paragraph breaks.

As part of its goal of "assembling a class that is both exceptionally academically qualified and broadly diverse," the Law School seeks to "enroll a 'critical mass' of minority students." Brief for Respondents Bollinger et al. 13. The Law School's interest is not simply "to assure within its student body some specified percentage of a particular group merely because of its race or ethnic origin." *Bakke*, 438 U.S., at 307 (opinion of Powell, J.). That would amount to outright racial balancing, which is patently unconstitutional. *Ibid.*; *Freeman v. Pitts*, 503 U.S. 467, 494 (1992) ("Racial balance is not to be achieved for its own sake"); *Richmond* v. *J. A. Croson Co.*, 488 U.S., at 507. Rather, the Law School's concept of critical mass is defined by reference to the educational benefits that diversity is designed to produce. These benefits are substantial. As the District Court emphasized, the Law School's admissions policy promotes "cross-racial understanding," helps to break down racial stereotypes, and "enables [students] to better understand persons of different races." App. to Pet. for Cert. 246a. These benefits are "important and laudable," because "classroom discussion is livelier, more spirited, and simply more enlightening and interesting" when the students have "the greatest possible variety of backgrounds." *Id.*, at 246a, 244a. The Law School's claim of a compelling interest is further bolstered by its *amici*, who point to the educational benefits that flow from student

body diversity. In addition to the expert studies and reports entered into evidence at trial, numerous studies show that student body diversity promotes learning outcomes, and "better prepares students for an increasingly diverse workforce and society, and better prepares them as professionals." Brief for American Educational Research Association et al. as *Amici Curiae* 3; see, *e.g.*, W. Bowen & D. Bok, The Shape of the River (1998); Diversity Challenged: Evidence on the Impact of Affirmative Action (G. Orfield & M. Kurlaender eds. 2001); Compelling Interest: Examining the Evidence on Racial Dynamics in Colleges and Universities (M. Chang, D. Witt, J. Jones, & K. Hakuta eds. 2003). These benefits are not theoretical but real, as major American businesses have made clear that the skills needed in today's increasingly global marketplace can only be developed through exposure to widely diverse people, cultures, ideas, and viewpoints. Brief for 3M et al. as *Amici Curiae* 5; Brief for General Motors Corp. as *Amicus Curiae* 3–4. What is more, high-ranking retired officers and civilian leaders of the United States military assert that, "[b]ased on [their] decades of experience," a "highly qualified, racially diverse officer corps . . . is essential to the military's ability to fulfill its principle mission to provide national security." Brief for Julius W. Becton, Jr. et al. as *Amici Curiae* 27. The primary sources for the Nation's officer corps are the service academies and the Reserve Officers Training Corps (ROTC), the latter comprising students already admitted to participating colleges and universities. *Id.*, at 5. At present, "the military cannot achieve an officer corps that is *both* highly qualified *and* racially diverse unless the service academies and the ROTC used limited race-conscious recruiting and admissions policies." *Ibid.* (emphasis in original). To fulfill its mission, the military "must be selective in admissions for training and education for the officer corps, *and* it must train and educate a highly qualified, racially diverse officer corps in a racially diverse setting." *Id.*, at 29 (emphasis in original). We agree that "[i]t requires only a small step from this analysis to conclude that our country's other most selective institutions must remain both diverse and selective." *Ibid.*

4. **Justice Clarence Thomas:** Justice Clarence Thomas was one of four justices who dissented in the *Grutter* case mentioned above. The lone Black justice on the court and someone whose personal experience with (and antipathy for) affirmative action is recounted in his 2007 memoir *My Grandfather's Son*, he opened his opinion the following way. Find the paragraph breaks.

> Frederick Douglass, speaking to a group of abolitionists almost 140 years ago, delivered a message lost on today's majority: "[I]n regard to the colored people, there is always more that is benevolent, I perceive, than just, manifested towards us. What I ask for the negro is not benevolence, not pity, not sympathy, but simply *justice.* The American people have always been anxious to know what they shall do with us. . . . I have had but one answer from the beginning. Do nothing with us! Your doing with us has already played the mischief with us. Do nothing with us! If the apples will not remain on the tree of their own strength, if they are worm-eaten at the core, if they are early ripe and disposed to fall, let them fall! . . . And if the negro cannot stand on his own legs, let him fall also. All I ask is, give him a chance to stand on his own legs! Let him alone! . . . [Y]our interference is doing him positive injury." What the Black Man Wants:

An Address Delivered in Boston, Massachusetts, on 26 January 1865, reprinted in 4 The Frederick Douglass Papers 59, 68 (J. Blassingame & J. McKivigan eds. 1991) (emphasis in original). Like Douglass, I believe blacks can achieve in every avenue of American life without the meddling

of university administrators. Because I wish to see all students succeed whatever their color, I share, in some respect, the sympathies of those who sponsor the type of discrimination advanced by the University of Michigan Law School (Law School). The Constitution does not, however, tolerate institutional devotion to the status quo in admissions policies when such devotion ripens into racial discrimination. Nor does the Constitution countenance the unprecedented deference the Court gives to the Law School, an approach inconsistent with the very concept of "strict scrutiny." No one would argue that a university could set up a lower general admission standard and then impose heightened requirements only on black applicants. Similarly, a university may not maintain a high admission standard and grant exemptions to favored races. The Law School, of its own choosing, and for its own purposes, maintains an exclusionary admissions system that it knows produces racially disproportionate results. Racial discrimination is not a permissible solution to the self-inflicted wounds of this elitist admissions policy. The majority upholds the Law School's racial discrimination not by interpreting the people's Constitution, but by responding to a faddish slogan of the cognoscenti. Nevertheless, I concur in part in the Court's opinion. First, I agree with the Court insofar as its decision, which approves of only one racial classification, confirms that further use of race in admissions remains unlawful. Second, I agree with the Court's holding that racial discrimination in higher education admissions will be illegal in 25 years. See *ante*, at 31 (stating that racial discrimination will no longer be narrowly tailored, or "necessary to further" a compelling state interest, in 25 years). I respectfully dissent from the remainder of the Court's opinion and the judgment, however, because I believe that the Law School's current use of race violates the Equal Protection Clause and that the Constitution means the same thing today as it will in 300 months.

5. **Stephen King:** Stephen King writes books at a pace at which most people would be happy to write emails. But after being injured in a terrible car accident in 1999, he struggled to regain his literary rhythm and had serious doubts about whether he would ever be able to finish another book. So he returned to a draft of a memoir he started a couple of years before the accident. That memoir later became the celebrated book *On Writing*, and King's prolific output soon returned. A section in *On Writing* about King's approach to paragraphs is below.

> I would argue that the paragraph, not the sentence, is the basic unit of writing—the place where coherence begins and words stand a chance of becoming more than mere words. If the moment of quickening is to come, it comes at the level of the paragraph. It is a marvelous and flexible instrument that can be a single word long or run on for pages (one paragraph in Don Robertson's historical novel *Paradise Falls* is sixteen pages long; there are paragraphs in Ross Lockridge's *Raintree Country* which are nearly that). You must learn to use it well if you are to write well. What this means is lots of practice; you have to learn the beat.

Answer Key

1. Philip Roth (*American Pastoral*)

The Swede. During the war years, when I was still a grade school boy, this was a magical name in our Newark neighborhood, even to adults just a generation removed from the city's old Prince Street ghetto and not yet so flawlessly Americanized as to be bowled over by the prowess of a high school athlete. The name was magical; so was the anomalous face. Of the few fair-complexioned Jewish students in our preponderantly Jewish public high school, none possessed anything remotely like the steep-jawed, insentient Viking mask of this blue-eyed blond born into our tribe as Seymour Irving Levov.

The Swede starred as end in football, center in basketball, and first baseman in baseball. Only the basketball team was ever any good—twice winning the city championship while he was its leading scorer—but as long as the Swede excelled, the fate of our sports teams didn't matter much to a student body whose elders, largely undereducated and overburdened, venerated academic achievement above all else. Physical aggression, even camouflaged by athletic uniforms and official rules and intended to do no harm to Jews, was not a traditional source of pleasure in our community—advanced degrees were. Nonetheless, through the Swede, the neighborhood entered into a fantasy about itself and about the world, the fantasy of sports fans everywhere: almost like Gentiles (as they imagined Gentiles), our families could forget the way things actually work and make an athletic performance the repository of all their hopes. Primarily, they could forget the war.

The elevation of Swede Levov into the household Apollo of the Weequahic Jews can best be explained, I think, by the war against the Germans and the Japanese and the fears that it fostered. With the Swede indomitable on the playing field, the meaningless surface of life provided a bizarre, delusionary kind of sustenance, the happy release into a Swedian innocence, for those who lived in dread of never seeing their sons or their brothers or their husbands again.

2. Philip Roth (Wikipedia Letter)

Dear Wikipedia,

I am Philip Roth. I had reason recently to read for the first time the Wikipedia entry discussing my novel "The Human Stain." The entry contains a serious misstatement that I would like to ask to have removed. This item entered Wikipedia not from the world of truthfulness but from the babble of literary gossip—there is no truth in it at all.

Yet when, through an official interlocutor, I recently petitioned Wikipedia to delete this misstatement, along with two others, my interlocutor was told by the "English Wikipedia Administrator"—in a letter dated August 25th and addressed to my interlocutor—that I, Roth, was not a credible source: "I understand your point that the author is the greatest authority on their own work," writes the Wikipedia Administrator—"but we require secondary sources."

Thus was created the occasion for this open letter. After failing to get a change made through the usual channels, I don't know how else to proceed.[*]

3. Justice Sandra Day O'Connor

As part of its goal of "assembling a class that is both exceptionally academically qualified and broadly diverse," the Law School seeks to "enroll a 'critical mass' of minority students." Brief for Respondents Bollinger et al. 13. The Law School's interest is not simply "to assure within its student body some specified percentage of a particular group merely because of its race or ethnic origin." *Bakke*, 438 U.S., at 307 (opinion of Powell, J.). That would amount to outright racial balancing, which is patently unconstitutional. *Ibid.*; *Freeman v. Pitts*, 503 U.S. 467, 494 (1992) ("Racial balance is not to be achieved for its own sake"); *Richmond v. J. A. Croson Co.*, 488 U.S., at 507. Rather, the Law School's concept of critical mass is defined by reference to the educational benefits that diversity is designed to produce.

These benefits are substantial. As the District Court emphasized, the Law School's admissions policy promotes "cross-racial understanding," helps to break down racial stereotypes, and "enables [students] to better understand persons of different races." App. to Pet. for

---

[*] The Wikipedia entry now contains a subsection titled "Alleged resemblance to Anatole Broyard," which states that certain reviews of the novel "suggested that the central character of Coleman Silk might have been inspired by Anatole Broyard." *The Human Stain*, Wikipedia (May 28, 2022, 4:32 UTC), https://en .wikipedia.org/w/index.php?title–The_Human_Stain&oldid=1090216004. The section concludes that Roth has stated he did not know of Broyard's ancestry until after the book was in progress.

Cert. 246a. These benefits are "important and laudable," because "classroom discussion is livelier, more spirited, and simply more enlightening and interesting" when the students have "the greatest possible variety of backgrounds." *Id.*, at 246a, 244a.

The Law School's claim of a compelling interest is further bolstered by its *amici*, who point to the educational benefits that flow from student body diversity. In addition to the expert studies and reports entered into evidence at trial, numerous studies show that student body diversity promotes learning outcomes, and "better prepares students for an increasingly diverse workforce and society, and better prepares them as professionals." Brief for American Educational Research Association et al. as *Amici Curiae* 3; see, *e.g.*, W. Bowen & D. Bok, The Shape of the River (1998); Diversity Challenged: Evidence on the Impact of Affirmative Action (G. Orfield & M. Kurlaender eds. 2001); Compelling Interest: Examining the Evidence on Racial Dynamics in Colleges and Universities (M. Chang, D. Witt, J. Jones, & K. Hakuta eds. 2003).

These benefits are not theoretical but real, as major American businesses have made clear that the skills needed in today's increasingly global marketplace can only be developed through exposure to widely diverse people, cultures, ideas, and viewpoints. Brief for 3M et al. as *Amici Curiae* 5; Brief for General Motors Corp. as *Amicus Curiae* 3–4. What is more, high-ranking retired officers and civilian leaders of the United States military assert that, "[b]ased on [their] decades of experience," a "highly qualified, racially diverse officer corps . . . is essential to the military's ability to fulfill its principle mission to provide national security." Brief for Julius W. Becton, Jr. et al. as *Amici Curiae* 27. The primary sources for the Nation's officer corps are the service academies and the Reserve Officers Training Corps (ROTC), the latter comprising students already admitted to participating colleges and universities. *Id.*, at 5. At present, "the military cannot achieve an officer corps that is *both* highly qualified *and* racially diverse unless the service academies and the ROTC used limited race-conscious recruiting and admissions policies." *Ibid.* (emphasis in original). To fulfill its mission, the military "must be selective in admissions for training and education for the officer corps, *and* it must train and educate a highly qualified, racially diverse officer corps in a racially diverse setting." *Id.*, at 29 (emphasis in original). We agree that "[i]t requires only a small step from this analysis to conclude that our country's other most selective institutions must remain both diverse and selective."

4. Justice Clarence Thomas

Frederick Douglass, speaking to a group of abolitionists almost 140 years ago, delivered a message lost on today's majority:

"[I]n regard to the colored people, there is always more that is benevolent, I perceive, than just, manifested towards us. What I ask for the negro is not benevolence, not pity, not sympathy, but simply *justice*. The American people have always been anxious to know what they shall do with us. . . . I have had but one answer from the beginning. Do nothing with us! Your doing with us has already played the mischief with us. Do nothing with us! If the apples will not remain on the tree of their own strength, if they are worm-eaten at the core, if they are early ripe and disposed to fall, let them fall! . . . And if the negro cannot stand on his own legs, let him fall also. All I ask is, give him a chance to stand on his own legs! Let him alone! . . . [Y]our interference is doing him positive injury." What the Black Man Wants: An Address Delivered in Boston, Massachusetts, on 26 January 1865, reprinted in 4 The Frederick Douglass Papers 59, 68 (J. Blassingame & J. McKivigan eds. 1991) (emphasis in original).

Like Douglass, I believe blacks can achieve in every avenue of American life without the meddling of university administrators. Because I wish to see all students succeed whatever their color, I share, in some respect, the sympathies of those who sponsor the type of discrimination advanced by the University of Michigan Law School (Law School). The Constitution does not, however, tolerate institutional devotion to the status quo in admissions policies when such devotion ripens into racial discrimination. Nor does the Constitution countenance the unprecedented deference the Court gives to the Law School, an approach inconsistent with the very concept of "strict scrutiny."

No one would argue that a university could set up a lower general admission standard and then impose heightened requirements only on black applicants. Similarly, a university may not maintain a high admission standard and grant exemptions to favored races.

The Law School, of its own choosing, and for its own purposes, maintains an exclusionary admissions system that it knows produces racially disproportionate results. Racial discrimination is not a permissible solution to the self-inflicted wounds of this elitist admissions policy. The majority upholds the Law School's racial discrimination not by interpreting the people's Constitution, but by responding to a faddish slogan of the cognoscenti. Nevertheless, I concur in part in the Court's opinion. First, I agree with the Court insofar as its decision, which approves of only one racial classification, confirms that further use of race in admissions remains unlawful. Second, I agree with the Court's holding that racial discrimination in higher education admissions will be illegal in 25 years. See *ante*, at 31 (stating that racial discrimination will no longer be narrowly tailored, or "necessary to further" a compelling state interest, in 25 years). I respectfully dissent from the remainder of the Court's opinion and the judgment, however, because I believe that the Law School's current use of race violates the Equal Protection Clause and that the Constitution means the same thing today as it will in 300 months.

5. Stephen King (*On Writing*)

Note: King decided to go without any paragraph breaks in the selected passage. It was all just one linked thought:

I would argue that the paragraph, not the sentence, is the basic unit of writing—the place where coherence begins and words stand a chance of becoming more than mere words. If the moment of quickening is to come, it comes at the level of the paragraph. It is a marvelous and flexible instrument that can be a single word long or run on for pages (one paragraph in Don Robertson's historical novel *Paradise Falls* is sixteen pages long; there are paragraphs in Ross Lockridge's *Raintree Country* which are nearly that). You must learn to use it well if you are to write well. What this means is lots of practice; you have to learn the beat.

High-Stakes Project: An Accumulation of Paragraphs

A book can be said to be an accumulation of paragraphs.
—Sol Stein, *Stein on Writing* (1995)

Background

In the High-Stakes Project section of the "Shot Selection" chapter, we gathered some data on the length and variety of your sentences. Now it's time to gather some data on the length and variety of your paragraphs.

Assignment

Step 1: Take a look at your high-stakes project.

Step 2: Find your longest paragraph. Count the number of lines.

Step 3: Find your shortest paragraph. Count the number of lines.

Step 4: Consider the following questions, which are very similar to the ones we asked in the "Shot Selection" chapter:

- Do you think your target audience will find your longest paragraph too long?
- Do you think your target audience will find your shortest paragraph too short?
- Do your other paragraphs more closely resemble your longest paragraph or your shortest paragraph?
- How does your paragraph range compare with the paragraph range of people you will be competing against or collaborating with? For example:
  - If you are trying to publish an Op-Ed in your local newspaper, how does your paragraph range compare with Op-Eds the paper has already published?
  - If you are trying to put together an investment prospectus, how does your paragraph range compare with the paragraph range in the prospectus of a company you admire?

○ If you are trying to complete a senior thesis, how does your paragraph range compare with the paragraph range of students who have won your department's award for best thesis?

Step 5 (optional): Repeat steps 1–4 for other projects you are working on, keeping in mind that a paragraph range that works well with a certain audience might not work well with a different audience. People who read your emails expect a different paragraphing style than people who read, say, a grant proposal you put together or a cover letter you send out.

Step 6 (optional): Take a look at the paragraph range of your text messages. Are you more of a "waterfall" type of texter (long messages, without any breaks between lines) or a "raindrop" type of texter (short, staccato messages, with breaks after essentially each thought)?

For more on this distinction, google the playfully informative essay "How Do You Text?" by Cecilia Watson, the author of *Semicolon: The Past, Present, and Future of a Misunderstood Mark*. In the meantime, here's a look at some of her advice:

- "If you're writing to a coworker or to someone you don't know well, mirroring more traditional paragraphing seems sensibly cautious, conveys respect and gives the recipient a sense that you think things through fully before sending."

- "If you're apologizing, sending condolences, or otherwise trying to convey something heartfelt via text message, it makes sense to [avoid the raindrop approach and] send your message all in one go. When the person you're texting is upset, a series of fragmented thoughts can ratchet up the emotional valence of your correspondence:

a staccato burst of texts sometimes resembles the heated outbursts characteristic of an in-person argument."

- "The same sense of emotion and spontaneity that can render the brevity and irregular rhythms of raindrop texts inappropriate for heavy-hitting messages can make them ideal for striking a playful and chatty tone, or for inviting feedback and conversation, like a ball casually tossed back and forth in a short arc. They are perfect for quick observations or reports on everyday life that don't require a response."

PART V

Reading, listening, even thinking, I was mesmerized by the sounds and the movement of words. Words could be sudden, like "jolt," or slow, like "meandering." Words could be sharp or smooth, cool, silvery, prickly to touch, blaring like a trumpet call, fluid, pitter-pattered in rhythm.

—Alan Lightman, *A Sense of the Mysterious: Science and the Human Spirit* (2005)

PREVIOUSLY ON

This will be our final section of Previously On. To reinforce why we regularly take these breaks to review and reflect, consider an observation made by the award-winning Harvard physics professor Eric Mazur, who has been a leading proponent of moving away from the standard "I lecture / You (passively) listen" model of instruction. "Education is much more than information transfer," he explains in a 2009 essay that advocates for, among other things, creating class time for students to process and contextualize what they've just been taught. "New information needs to be connected to old information in the student's mind."

A similar recommendation was made all the way back in 1933 by the American philosopher John Dewey, who devoted much of his life to improving the structure of education and even helped create an experimental "lab school" on the campus of the University of Chicago that has developed into one of the most prestigious K–12 programs in the country. (The daughters of Barack and Michelle Obama went there when the family still lived in Chicago.) "Of course intellectual learning includes the amassing and retention of information," according to Dewey. "But information is an undigested burden unless it is understood." He goes on to say that true understanding "is attained only when acquisition is accompanied by constant reflection upon the meaning of what is studied."

Consumption, in other words, isn't enough. What's needed is a more active form of processing. We can't expect to retain insights, much less produce them, if we don't regularly set aside time to think about and file the new material we've recently absorbed.

With that in mind, take a shot at the next set of questions. Each requires you to apply the definitions we covered in the "Spotting Sentences" chapter—*simple, compound, complex, compound-complex*—to short statements that evoke concepts from other chapters. The goal is to create a helpful kind of double review.

Questions

Identify whether the statement is an example of a simple sentence, a compound sentence, a complex sentence, or a compound-complex sentence. If there are multiple sentences in the passage, answer based on the underlined portion.

1. "Editing and Empathy" (Chapter 1)

"The reader is out there, and she is real. She's interested in life and, by picking up our work, has given us the benefit of the doubt. All we have to do is engage her. To engage her, all we have to do is value her."

—George Saunders, *Swimming in a Pond in the Rain* (2021)

A. simple
B. compound
C. complex
D. compound-complex

2. "Editing and Interleaving" (Chapter 2)

"Your artist's mind is always working, even when you think it's idling. In the studio, even doing nothing can be a form of working. This is also true when you're out walking, traveling, worrying, staying awake all night, whatever. *All* these things will be part of your work."

—Jerry Salz, *How to Be an Artist* (2020)

    A. simple
    B. compound
    C. complex
    D. compound-complex

3. "Map to a Decision" (Chapter 5)

"<u>If you plan to travel after dark, you'd better hope that you aren't in the Southern Hemisphere, which has no equivalent of the North Star, or you'd better be able to rival Galileo with your knowledge of the nightly and seasonal course of the constellations.</u> But, even if all this applied, you would still be in trouble if you did not also have a map."

—Kathryn Schulz, "Why Animals Don't Get Lost" (2021)

    A. simple
    B. compound
    C. complex
    D. compound-complex

4. "Shot Selection" (Chapter 7)

"Variation is the life of prose."

—Verlyn Klinkenborg, *Several Short Sentences about Writing* (2012)

    A. simple
    B. compound
    C. complex
    D. compound-complex

5. "Paragraphing" (Chapter 8)

"Their style was periodic, and their unit was the fully crafted paragraph."

—Description of the writing style of the historian Edward Gibbon and the literary critic Samuel Johnson by Leo Damrosch in *The Club: Johnson, Boswell, and the Friends Who Shaped an Age* (2019)

A. simple
B. compound
C. complex
D. compound-complex

Answer Key

1. **B. Compound.** The underlined portion from George Saunders's book is a compound sentence. The first part ("The reader is out there") is simple; it's just one independent clause. The second part ("she is real") is another independent clause. So the combination of the two parts creates a compound sentence. Here's the sentence again if you want to take a second look: "The reader is out there, and she is real."

2. **C. Complex.** The underlined portion from Jerry Salz's book is a complex sentence. The first part ("Your artist's mind is always working") is simple. It is an independent clause. The second part ("even when you think it's idling") is a dependent clause. As a result, the full sentence is complex. Here's the sentence again if you want to take a second look: "Your artist's mind is always working, even when you think it's idling."

3. **D. Compound-complex.** The underlined portion from Kathryn Schulz's article is a compound-complex sentence. The first part ("If you plan . . . North Star") is complex. It has a dependent clause and an independent clause. The second part ("you'd better be able to . . .") is another independent clause. Together, the two parts create a compound-complex sentence. Here's the sentence again if you want to take a second look: "If you plan to travel after dark, you'd better hope that you aren't in the Southern Hemisphere, which has no equivalent of the North Star, or you'd better be able to rival Galileo with your knowledge of the nightly and seasonal course of the constellations."

4. **B. Compound.** The passage from Verlyn Klinkenborg's book is a simple sentence. The sentence is an independent

clause. Here it is again if you want to take a second look: "Variation is the life of prose."

5. **B. Compound.** The passage from Leo Damrosch's book is a compound sentence. The first part ("Their style was periodic") is simple; it's just one independent clause. The second part ("their unit was . . . paragraph") is another independent clause, creating a compound sentence. Here's the sentence again if you want to take a second look: "Their style was periodic, and their unit was the fully crafted paragraph."

CHAPTER 9

Rhetorical Repetition

Journalists and schoolteachers mean well, but they can be fatally bossy. One of their strangely arbitrary rules forbids us to use the same word twice on the same page. Thus they drive us to the thesaurus in desperate searches for far-fetched synonyms and substitutes.

—Ursula K. Le Guin, *Steering the Craft* (1998)

Just because you have used a word doesn't mean you can't use it again, perhaps even in the same sentence. Marketers understand this point well. The repetition of the word "Vegas" in the city's promotional slogan "What happens in <u>Vegas</u>, stays in <u>Vegas</u>" is not an accident. Nor is the repetition used by two companies that likely sell a lot of drinks in that city.

Hennessy: <u>Never</u> stop. <u>Never</u> settle.
Heineken: <u>Open</u> your mind. <u>Open</u> your world.

Yet when it comes to selling ideas—whether to judges, boardrooms, or even just to a coworker—many advocates shy away from repetition. They remain committed to the idea, often developed in college, that good writing is associated with having (and showing) a big vocabulary. They mistakenly think the best thesaurus wins.

This prejudice is not particularly new. In the first decades of the 20th century, the renowned lexicographer Henry Watson Fowler complained about a phenomenon he pejoratively called "elegant variation": overusing synonyms on the misguided belief that variety beats clarity. "It is the second-rate writers," he writes in *A Dictionary of Modern English Usage*, "those intent on expressing themselves prettily rather than on conveying their meaning clearly, & still more those whose notions of style are based on a few misleading rules of thumb, that are chiefly open to the allurement of elegant variation." Below is one of his examples:

Rarely does the "Little Summer" linger until **November**, but at times its stay has been prolonged until quite late in **the year's penultimate month**.

There's no need to reidentify November as "the year's penultimate month" in that sentence. It would be like saying, "What happens in Vegas, stays in Sin City." The synonym is unnecessary, even confusing.

These types of pitfalls help explain why the language maven Bryan Garner insists on calling elegant variation "inelegant variation." "Variety for variety's sake in word choice can confuse readers," he writes in his own Fowler-like usage dictionary, *Garner's Modern English Usage*. "If you write about a person's 'candor' in one sentence and 'honesty' in the next, is the reader to infer that you are distinguishing between two traits, or using different words to refer to the same one?" The answer is not immediately clear.

The stakes are even higher, Garner notes, in legal writing: "If different words are used, different meanings must have been intended." Here's one of the unreformed examples he gives in his more law-specific usage dictionary, *A Dictionary of Modern Legal Usage*:

> State law makes no provisions for mandatory *autopsies*, which means that justices of the peace follow different policies for seeking *post-mortems*.

The words "autopsies" and "post-mortems" are meant to indicate the same thing, but the switch in terminology injects some unhelpful ambiguity into the sentence. A similar hiccup occurs in a second example:

> *Lawyers* generally have a bad reputation; today the American public holds a grudge against the half-million *counselors* who handle its legal affairs.

Is a "lawyer" the same as a "counselor"? Given the sentence's imprecision, readers can be forgiven for being unsure.

A. Awkward Repetition: "Take Care of the Situation"

I don't mean to imply that repetition is always preferred. One of the most frequent comments I make on the legal briefs I edit is "awkward repetition." A pair of sentences from an appellate brief written by a student in the University of Michigan Workers' Rights Clinic—which is a group of faculty and students who take on a wide range of employment law cases pro bono—offers a good starting point. The first sentence in the pair highlights that a supervisor named Mr. Harve pledged to address the sexual harassment the student's client had been enduring from coworkers. Note the student's use of the phrase "take care of the situation":

> Mr. Harve promised he would take care of the situation.

The problem is that the student repeats the same phrase in the very next sentence, as you can see when the two sentences are grouped together.

> Mr. Harve promised he would <u>take care of the situation</u>. He said he would wait at the workstation at the start of the shift the next day and "<u>take care of the situation</u> so the abuse never happened again."

That's awkward. It's almost as if the student wrote the second sentence without remembering the words they put in the first. Here's a different approach:

> Mr. Harve promised he would take care of the situation. He said he would wait at the workstation at the start of the shift the next day and make sure "the abuse never happened again."

This edit eliminates the awkward repetition. It also has the added benefit of condensing the quotation, a step that lets readers focus on a tidier passage of text. That's usually a good thing. Nobody wants to read words they don't need to—especially when those words are ones they have already read.

B. Awkward Repetition: "Law School"

A second example shows that awkward repetition can contaminate not just pairs of sentences but single sentences as well. The example comes from a cover letter written by a law student seeking an internship at the Securities Exchange Commission (or "SEC") in New York. You don't need to read the whole sentence to spot the problem:

> In <u>law school</u>, I have enjoyed my <u>law school</u> classes . . .

That's redundant. There's no reason to include "law school" a second time. The phrase doesn't add anything new or helpful. It just takes up space.

To his credit, the student quickly realized his mistake once I asked him to read the sentence out loud. He took out "my law school" and just went with "In law school, I have enjoyed classes such as. . . ." That improved things considerably.

It also reinforced a lesson I try to pass on to all my students: among the many benefits of reading your writing out loud is that it can help you distinguish between awkward repetition and rhetorical repetition. By "rhetorical repetition," I mean those intentional bits of repetition that add helpful rhythm and force to your words. "Anaphora" is the term for when this repetition comes at the beginning of successive sentences, phrases, or clauses. Here's Justice Sonia Sotomayor using it in an impassioned dissent:

> <u>Race matters</u> to a young man's view of society when he spends his teenage years watching others tense up as he passes, no matter the neighborhood where he grew up. <u>Race matters</u> to a young woman's sense of self when she states her hometown, and then is pressed, "No, where are you really from?," regardless of how many generations

her family has been in the country. <u>Race matters</u> to a young person addressed by a stranger in a foreign language, which he does not understand because only English was spoken at home. <u>Race matters</u> because of the slights, the snickers, the silent judgments that reinforce that most crippling of thoughts: "I do not belong here."

"Epistrophe," on the other hand, is the term for when intentional repetition comes at the end of successive sentences, phrases, or clauses. One of the more famous Supreme Court opinions of all time, *McCulloch v. Maryland*, has a good example courtesy of Chief Justice John Marshall:

> If any one proposition could command the universal assent of mankind, we might expect it would be this—that the Government of the Union, though limited in its powers, is supreme within its sphere of action. This would seem to result necessarily from its nature. It is the Government of <u>all</u>; its powers are delegated by <u>all</u>; it represents <u>all</u>, and acts for <u>all</u>.

Some students have a hard time remembering the word "anaphora." Others have a hard time remembering "epistrophe." Both, to me, sound more like the names of perfumes than like a writing move I'd want to use. So I tend to place each of them under the broad banner of the term I used before: "rhetorical repetition."

But if you find value in the lexical precision that the labels "anaphora" and "epistrophe" provide, definitely use them. They may help you remember that rhetorical repetition can work well (1) at the beginning of a construction, (2) at the end of a construction, and (3) sometimes even at both the beginning of a construction *and* the end of a construction, as the advertising legend David Ogilvy shows in the sentence below:

A special problem with the employees of an advertising agency is that each one watches the other one very carefully **to see if one** gets a carpet <u>before the other</u>, **to see if one** has an assistant <u>before the other</u>, or **to see if one** makes an extra nickel <u>before the other</u>.

To help give you a sense of the wider range of compositional choices available, the Low-Stakes Practice section of this chapter includes several additional examples of skillful uses of rhetorical repetition. You'll then have a chance, in the High-Stakes Project section, to review your own writing to see if you can spot and replace any instances of awkward repetition.

There isn't always an easy way to articulate what distinguishes rhetorical repetition from awkward repetition, but one step is to ask, Did the writer repeat the word or phrase on purpose? If you don't think they did, that's a pretty good sign that it's awkward repetition, especially if the words sound clumsy when read out loud.

Which means the rhetorical repetition Justice Potter Stewart famously used when explaining how to spot obscenity—"I know it when I see it"—might also, in a slightly modified form, serve as a good standard for catching awkward repetition: "I know it when I *hear* it."

Awkward Repetition

1. "<u>Both</u> restrictions are <u>both</u> quite broad."

   —Memo by a first-year law student

2. "The league was for 14–16 year olds. Felicia was the youngest player. Team tryouts are very competitive. Being selected for the league gave her confidence <u>after</u> having difficulty making friends in school <u>after</u> moving."

   —Memo by a first-year law student

3. "In applying the susceptibility standard, we need to learn if Shrecklich was aware of Cindy's susceptibilities and

whether his comments were intended to <u>address</u> them. Two facts <u>address</u> this issue."

—Memo by a first-year law student

4. "It is clear that there is <u>still</u> a lot of work that needs to be done. Vacant buildings, crime, and foreclosures <u>still</u> exist."

—Cover letter by a first-year law student

5. "Even in the face of challenges posed by the fact that Mr. Prent's mother was battling cancer, he was <u>promoted</u> to a program coordinator position. He was placed on a team in charge of public outreach and helped develop policy initiatives and <u>promotional</u> materials used by the agency to interact with the public."

—Memo by a first-year law student

Rhetorical Repetition

1. "The beginnings of confusion with us in England are at present feeble enough, but with you in France we have seen an even more feeble infancy growing rapidly into a strength to heap mountains on mountains and to wage war with heaven itself. When our neighbour's house is on fire, it can't be wrong to have the fire-engines to play a little on our own. Better to be despised for <u>undue</u> anxiety than ruined by <u>undue</u> confidence."

—Edmund Burke, Reflections on the
Revolution in France (1790)

2. "I couldn't stand fish; <u>boiled</u> cod, which we had at least once a week, made me feel nauseous, as did the steam from the pain in which it was cooked, its taste and consistency. I felt the same about <u>boiled</u> pollock, <u>boiled</u> coley, <u>boiled</u> haddock, <u>boiled</u> flounder, <u>boiled</u> mackerel, and <u>boiled</u> rose fish."

—Karl Ove Knausgaard, My Struggle: Book One (2013)

3. "<u>We did not know</u> **how many** survivors wanted us to represent them. <u>We did not know</u> **how many** of the survivors would be seeking compensation for the death of family or relatives, **how many** would be seeking recovery only for lost cars or houses, **how many** would be seeking recovery for injuries. <u>We didn't even know</u> whom to sue."
   —Gerald Stern, *The Buffalo Creek Disaster: How the Survivors of One of the Worst Disasters in Coal-Mining History Brought Suit against the Coal Company—and Won* (1976)

4. "<u>You are not mistaken</u> in believing that drugs are a scourge that is devastating our society. <u>You are not mistaken</u> in believing that drugs are tearing asunder our social fabric, ruining the lives of many young people, and imposing heavy costs on some of the most disadvantaged among us. <u>You are not mistaken</u> in believing that the majority of the public share your concerns. In short, <u>you are not mistaken</u> in the end you seek to achieve.

   Your mistake is failing to recognize that the very measures you favor are a major source of the evils you deplore."
   —Milton Friedman, "An Open Letter to Bill Bennett" (1989)

5. "It is a peculiar sensation, this double-consciousness, this sense of always looking at one's self through the eyes of others, of measuring one's soul by the tape of a world that looks on in amused contempt and pity. One ever feels his twoness,—an American, a Negro; <u>two</u> souls, <u>two</u> thoughts, <u>two</u> unreconciled strivings; <u>two</u> warring ideals in one dark body, whose dogged strength alone keeps it from being torn asunder."
   —W. E. B. Du Bois, *The Souls of Black Folk* (1903)

Low-Stakes Practice: Anaphora and Epistrophe

See One. Do One. Teach One.

—Learning plan for new surgeons

The Vocabulary part of the chapter introduced two forms of rhetorical repetition: "anaphora" and "epistrophe." Test your understanding of these terms by identifying which one best describes the passages below. If neither of them does, pick "neither" as your answer:

1. "Why am I compelled to write? Because the writing saves me from this complacency I fear. Because I have no choice. Because I must keep the spirit of my revolt and myself alive. Because the world I create in the writing compensates for what the real world does not give me."

   —Gloria Anzaldúa, "Speaking in Tongues: A Letter to Third World Women Writers" (2009)

   A. anaphora
   B. epistrophe
   C. neither

2. "Here I am, standing outside my home, looking out at the sky as the clouds gather and hide the rest of the universe. Here I am, a modern human with a mug made from the Earth, thinking about the complexities of the universe. The patterns are all around me, and I can touch them for myself."

   —Helen Czerski, *Storm in a Teacup: The Physics of Everyday Life* (2017)

   A. anaphora
   B. epistrophe
   C. neither

3. "A thing may be necessary, very necessary, absolutely or indispensably necessary."

> —Chief Justice John Marshall,
> *McCulloch v. Maryland* (1819)

A. anaphora
B. epistrophe
C. neither

4. "In Vienna, the little cakes looked like big buildings, or else the big buildings looked like little cakes. She ate both, layer upon layer."

   —Patricia Lockwood, *No One Is Talking about This* (2021)

A. anaphora
B. epistrophe
C. neither

Answer Key

1. **A.** The passage from Gloria Anzaldúa is an example of anaphora. Anzaldúa repeats the word "Because" at the beginning of four straight sentences: "<u>Because</u> the writing saves me from this complacency I fear. <u>Because</u> I have no choice. <u>Because</u> I must keep the spirit of my revolt and myself alive. <u>Because</u> the world I create in the writing compensates for what the real world does not give me."

2. **A.** The passage from Helen Czerski is an example of anaphora. Czerski repeats the word "Here" at the beginning of the first two sentences: "<u>Here</u> I am, standing outside my home, looking out at the sky as the clouds gather and hide the rest of the universe. <u>Here</u> I am, a modern human with a mug made from the Earth, thinking about the complexities of the universe."

3. **B.** The passage from Chief Justice John Marshall is an example of epistrophe. He repeats the word "necessary" at the end of successive phrases: "A thing may be <u>necessary</u>, very <u>necessary</u>, absolutely or indispensably <u>necessary</u>."

4. **C.** The passage from Patricia Lockwood is tricky. I wouldn't classify it as either anaphora or epistrophe. The first bit of rhetorical repetition—"the <u>little cakes</u> looked like *big buildings*, or else the *big buildings* looked like <u>little cakes</u>"—has its own name: "chiasmus." It's when you invert the order of words in an A-B-B-A way. As for the second bit of rhetorical repetition— "<u>layer</u> upon <u>layer</u>"—that move, in my view, is simply a general form of repetition, like the phrase "year after year" or "time after time." But if you picked anaphora or epistrophe for this answer, that's okay. The important thing is that you are starting to recognize when rhetorical repetition is skillfully deployed. The more you can do that, the more you'll be able to spot opportunities when you can skillfully deploy it yourself.

High-Stakes Project: Content Cleaning

Have any of you young ladies seen this young lady in the ladies'?

—Walter Tevis, *The Queen's Gambit* (1983)

Background

The Vocabulary section of this chapter noted that it can sometimes be hard to distinguish between rhetorical repetition and awkward repetition. The suggested test was to ask the following question: Did the writer repeat the word or phrase on purpose?

Assignment

Review your high-stakes project for opportunities where you can do at least one of the following:

- Enhance your content by inserting some rhetorical repetition.
- Clean up your content by eliminating awkward repetition.

Here are three additional examples of rhetorical repetition to increase your mental menu of options:

> **Judicial Opinion:** "<u>Even if</u> the defendant would suffer minimal or no inconvenience from being forced to litigate before the tribunals of another State; <u>even if</u> the forum State has a strong interest in applying its law to the controversy; <u>even if</u> the forum State is the most convenient location for litigation, the Due Process Clause, acting as an instrument of interstate federalism, may sometimes act to divest the State of its power to render a valid judgment."
>
> —Justice Byron White, *World-Wide Volkswagen Corp. v. Woodson* (1980)

Marketing Campaign: "Where <u>there is</u> a team, <u>there is</u> a way."
—Ad for Microsoft Teams* (2021)

Personal Essay: "I left the hospital at eleven that night. A few miles from my house, a motorcycle had overturned on the highway, catapulting a helmetless young man into space. Someone had lit a string of flares around the accident to divert traffic. The windows of my cab had been sandblasted into a sea-glass dullness by the city's famously abrasive winds, and the scene outside looked weirdly like some kind of celebration—a festival or a wedding party—shot through a foggy video camera. The inversion almost made me want to laugh. Delhi had landed upside down. The city <u>was broken</u>. This hospital <u>was broken</u>. My father <u>was broken</u>."
—Siddhartha Mukherjee, "My Father's Body, at Rest and in Motion" (2018)

As for awkward repetition, I have labeled below some common mistakes to look out for in your own writing:

Same Pronoun, Different Meaning: "To the extent that the requirement of diversity implies the possibility of national bias, <u>it</u> certainly doesn't condone <u>it</u>." *(The first "it" refers to "the requirement." But the second "it" confusingly refers to something else: "national bias.")*
—Draft of a legal brief by a second-year law student (2020)

Same Word, Different Form: <u>Designed</u> and led "<u>Design</u> Thinking Workshops"
—Résumé of a first-year law student (2020)

---

* Note how Microsoft's slogan plays off another example of rhetorical repetition: the saying "Where <u>there is a</u> will, <u>there is a</u> way."

Same Word, Different Meaning: "To succeed in law, business, education, government, health care, and many other fields, it is becoming increasingly important to distinguish yourself as a savvy communicator. Social media has only accelerated the ways in which we all must learn to use our words to connect, compete, and create. <u>Yet</u> there are features of the English language that many of us haven't taken full advantage of <u>yet</u>. *Notes on Nuance* is designed to help change that."

—Description on the back of the book
Notes on Nuance (2020)

I include that last example—where "yet" is used as a conjunction in the beginning of the sentence but is then used as an adverb at the end of the sentence—to highlight how I, myself, definitely fall victim to awkward repetition at times. I wrote that book description. I reviewed that book description. And when the book was officially published, that actually *was* the book description. I didn't realize how clumsy and inelegant the double "yet" was until several weeks later.

Fortunately, the publisher of the book was kind enough to make the change. But you might not be as lucky, so definitely try to rid your high-stakes project of similar sloppiness. Rhetorical repetition can help your audience notice connections between ideas. Awkward repetition usually just annoys them.

CHAPTER 10

Un-numb the Numbers

My relationship with statistics changed when I became one.

—Paul Kalanithi, *When Breath Becomes Air* (2016)

Numbers can be numbing. Depend too much on them to make your case, pitch your product, or tell your story, and you risk losing your audience. As Jay Conger puts it in "The Necessary Art of Persuasion," an article published in the *Harvard Business Review* in 1998, "Ordinary evidence . . . won't do. We have found that the most effective persuaders use language in a particular way. They supplement numerical data with examples, stories, metaphors, and analogies to make their positions come alive." This strategic use of language, Conger observes, "paints a vivid word picture, and, in doing so, lends a compelling and tangible quality to the persuader's point of view."

I explain this idea to my law students by offering the following bit of advice: if you are going to use some statistics as you argue or present, try to "un-numb the numbers."

Below are some examples of lawyers and other professionals skillfully using that technique.

A. Texas

We'll start with the basic move of putting a large and sometimes difficult-to-comprehend number in perspective. One hundred ninety million acres sounds like a lot of land. But without a reference point, it's tough to know just how much space that actually covers. So when US Supreme Court justice Antonin Scalia wrote the majority opinion in *Summers v. Earth Island Institute*, which involved the right to challenge US Forest Service regulations, he compared 190 million acres to something much more vivid and recognizable: the state of Texas.

"The National Forests occupy more than 190 million acres," he wrote, "an area larger than Texas."

The sentence wasn't a throwaway line. It was actually central to the court's decision in that case. Finding that the Earth Island Institute lacked the ability—or what is technically called "standing"—to even bring its claims, Scalia pointed out that the alleged injury involved one institute member's extremely vague plans to visit various national forests in the future. "There may be a chance, but it is hardly a likelihood, that [the member's] wanderings will bring him to a parcel about to be affected by a project unlawfully subject to the regulations," Scalia explained. "Indeed, without further specification it is impossible to tell *which* projects are . . . unlawfully subject to the regulations."

The Texas comparison made Scalia's analysis concrete and memorable. In his view, the Earth Island Institute was essentially basing its claim on the chance that one of its members would someday stumble across a certain parcel of land while wandering around a space the size of Texas. That's not nearly enough to qualify for legal relief, given that the required harm in this context needed to be "actual or imminent." "Accepting an intention to visit the National Forests as adequate to confer standing to challenge any Government action affecting any portion of those forests," Scalia wrote, summing up the case, "would be tantamount to eliminating the requirement of concrete, particularized injury in fact."

What the Texas visual did was to put the issue of the case in perspective. It gave it shape and dimensions. Too often we neglect this important step, especially if we have expertise in a particular field. We wrongly assume that our data and statistics will be self-explanatory. We don't realize that, in many cases, these numbers can be unhelpfully numbing.

B. Aspirin, Bicycles, and Fighter Jets

An expert who doesn't make this mistake is my office neighbor at the University of Michigan Law School, Nicholson Price. In addition to a law degree, Price has a PhD in biological sciences. The combination could lead to some dense, jargon-heavy writing. But Price does an admirable job of making his many scholarly papers as readable as they are rigorous. One in particular, which he coauthored with Arti Rai of Duke University School of Law, is a good example of how the importance of un-numbing the numbers extends beyond dealing with big numbers; it also arises when dealing with small numbers, or at least small-scale objects. Like atoms.

Here's the paper's opening paragraph:

> Most drugs are small. Aspirin, for instance, is made up of just 21 atoms. Small drugs like aspirin provide the majority of global revenue for brand-name drug companies. But finding new small-molecule drugs keeps getting harder, and generic drug manufacturers are quick to compete with brand-name firms once patents expire. As a result, drug companies are increasingly turning to very large drugs: biologics produced by living cells. In terms of size and rough complexity, if an aspirin were a bicycle, a small biologic would be a Toyota Prius, and a large biologic would be an F-16 fighter jet.

That last sentence—about bicycles, Priuses, and fighter jets—does a great job communicating a comparison that many readers might otherwise find difficult to grasp, especially if they have never heard of "biologics." Price and his coauthor don't dumb their material down. They enhance it by making it more vivid and accessible. They add value by using their rhetorical imagination.

We'd all benefit from developing that skill.

C. Justice as Translation

I tried to stress this point about imagination when I ran a workshop in a course Price was teaching on patent law one semester. We were trying to get the students to understand that at the heart of "un-numbing the numbers" is a core lawyerly skill: the skill of translation.

Another Michigan Law faculty member, James Boyd White, has even argued that the act of translation is at the very center of law. His 1994 book *Justice as Translation* lays out an elegant case for the deep parallels between translating a text and conducting yourself as a lawyer. Both give you a chance to learn a different language. For lawyers, this might mean learning the language of a client, the language of a contract, or the language of a whole new practice area.

Both also help you see the gaps in your own language, particularly while trying to capture somebody else's words or experience. As a result, you are continually faced with an important ethical test: Are you willing to take responsibility for the interpretive choices you make?

These and other insights prompted one reviewer of *Justice as Translation* to suggest that, solely on the strength of the book, "James Boyd White should be nominated for a seat on the Supreme Court."

The ambitions that Price and I had for the patent law workshop were considerably more modest. We simply wanted the students to understand the mechanics of a certain kind of translation: putting numbers in context.

In this way, we were following the lead of Chip Heath of Stanford University and Dan Heath of Duke University, who devote a significant portion of their best-selling book *Made to Stick* to the problem of communicating statistics. "Since grade school," they write, "we've been taught to support our arguments with statistical evidence. But statistics tend to be eye-glazing. How can we use them while still managing to engage our audience?"

The Heath brothers don't offer any failproof formula. Nor do I think one exists. But the strategies they identify go a long way toward helping people deliver numbers a little less numbingly. The next two sections of this essay, "Relationships" and "Human Element," summarize their approach.

D. Relationships

The first step is to remember that statistics are "rarely meaningful in and of themselves. Statistics will, and should, almost always be used to illustrate a *relationship*. It's more important for people to remember the relationship than the number."

Price's aspirin analogy is a great example. The critical point is not that the size of aspirin is just twenty-one atoms. The critical point is the relationship between the relatively small and simple structure of aspirin and the much larger and more complex structure of biologics. So long as readers understand that relationship, so long as they keep Price's three images in their heads—a bicycle (aspirin), a Toyota Prius (small biologic), and an F-16 fighter jet (large biologic)—they'll be fine.

Or take a different example, this time from another writing pair: Barry Nalebuff, who teaches at the Yale School of Management, and Ian Ayres, who teaches at Yale Law School. In their book *Why Not? How to Use Everyday Ingenuity to Solve Problems Big and Small*, Nalebuff and Ayres make the point that driving a car is "one of the most dangerous things we do." To support this claim, they cite two statistics: "In the United States there are 24 million auto accidents each year and 2.3 million people injured." But then, instead of citing a third statistic, at least in number form, they skip to a much more memorable relationship: "The number of auto fatalities is the equivalent of a 737 plane crash every day."

It's a common move: taking a big, tough-to-comprehend death toll and trying to put it in more concrete, memorable terms. Here's how the Civil War historian Allen Guelzo does it in *Gettysburg*, after acknowledging that numbers don't fully capture the experience of that epic battle. He's describing the losses endured by General Robert E. Lee and the Confederates. "Any way the numbers are piled, . . . the results were equivalent to a historic catastrophe. Even if one takes the lowest mark, the Army of Northern Virginia suffered something comparable to two sinkings of the *Titanic*, the 2001 attacks on the World Trade Center and the Pentagon, ten repetitions of the Great Blizzard of 1888, and two Pearl Harbors. Or, if percentages provide more clarity, the Confederates at Gettysburg sustained two and a half times the losses taken by the Allied armies in Normandy from D-Day through August 1944."

Guelzo then adds that anyone who has doubts about the impact of Gettysburg need only consult a letter that a Confederate soldier wrote to his sister soon after the battle ended. "The campaign is a

BATTLE OF GETTYSBURG
ON THIS FAMOUS FIELD WAS FOUGHT THE CRISIS BATTLE OF THE CIVIL WAR, EACH ARMY BEING 100,000 STRONG, THE CONFEDERATES UNDER GENERAL ROBERT E. LEE AND THE UNION FORCES UNDER GENERAL GEORGE G. MEADE. BOTH SIDES LOST MORE THAN A THIRD OF THEIR ENTIRE NUMBER

failure," the soldier lamented, "and the worst failure that the South has ever made."

E. Human Element

Guelzo's inclusion of the soldier's letter aligns well with the second strategy that the Heath brothers suggest: "Contextualize [statistics] in terms that are more human, more everyday." As an example, they offer the following sentences, which have slightly different wording but convey the same core information:

1. "Scientists recently computed an important physical constraint to an extraordinary accuracy. To put the accuracy in perspective,

imagine throwing a rock from the sun to the earth and hitting the target within one third of a mile of dead center."

2. "Scientists recently computed an important physical constraint to an extraordinary accuracy. To put the accuracy in perspective, imagine throwing a rock from New York to Los Angeles and hitting the target within two thirds of an inch of dead center."

"When different groups evaluated the two statements," they explain, "58 percent of respondents ranked the statistic about the sun to the earth as 'very impressive.' That jumped to 83 percent for the statistic about New York to Los Angeles." The reason for this discrepancy is that "we have no human experience, no intuition, about the distance between the sun and the earth. The distance from New York to Los Angeles is much more tangible."

The same could be said about Price's aspirin analogy. In fact, the idea of adding a human element to your statistics nicely complements the idea of establishing a memorable relationship. The two strategies are not mutually exclusive. A final example, from the energy company Opower, reinforces the point.

F. Opower

The story of Opower has been told in many places, including a case study used to teach MBA students about entrepreneurship and product development. The best account for our purposes comes in *Invisible Influence* by Wharton's Jonah Berger—if only because Berger himself does such a great job of un-numbing key numbers when giving it.

Berger begins by outlining Opower's basic approach, which uses social influence to help people reduce their energy consumption. The company's founders, David Yates and Adam Lasky, got the idea from an experiment conducted in San Marcos, California by the renowned psychologist Robert Cialdini and a team of graduate students. Just telling people that they would save money by using less energy in their homes didn't work very well. Nor did appeals to protecting the environment or being a responsible citizen. What worked was high-lighting social norms. "When surveyed, 77% of your neighbors use fans instead of air-conditioning to keep cool in the summer," the successful appeal read. "Turn off your air conditioning and turn on your fans."

People who received that message, Berger explains, "decreased their energy use significantly. And this reduced consumption per-sisted even weeks after they received the last appeal. Simply telling people that their neighbors were saving energy led them to conserve more themselves."

Keeping this study and Cialdini's other work in mind, the Opower founders teamed up with a number of utility companies to change the information that consumers received in their energy bills each month. No longer would a bill show just contextless data about the number of watts you used since your last payment. Now it would show your consumption relative to similar households in your neighborhood. The company figured out how to un-numb the numbers in a way that successfully changed people's behavior. Berger shares the specifics:

> These programs lead people to reduce their energy consumption by around 2 percent. For a given person, this decrease may not seem huge, but aggregated across the country the impact is staggering. Since their launch, Opower's programs have helped save more than 6 terawatt-hours of energy. That's 6 trillion watt-hours, or the equiva-lent to taking all the homes in Alaska and Hawaii, more than 2.1 mil-lion people, off the power grid for an entire year.

No wonder the software giant Oracle acquired the company in 2016 for over $500 million. Opower's ingenuity can really help with one of the most important numbers of all: the bottom line.

Low-Stakes Practice: Kansas and Calories

The Nanded hospital, however, is the lone public hospital serving a district of 1,400 villages like Uti, a population of 2.3 million people. It has five hundred beds, three main operating rooms, and, I found when I visited, just nine general surgeons. (Imagine Kansas with just nine surgeons.)

—Atul Gawande, *Better: A Surgeon's Notes on Performance* (2007)

Background

In "The Making of a Scientist," the Nobel Prize–winning physicist Richard Feynman tells a neat story about dinosaurs, the *Encyclopedia Britannica,* and an important lesson passed along to him by his father: when you are trying to communicate information, translate it into something concrete and memorable. The technique Feynman's father used to teach him this lesson is exactly what we've been learning to do in this chapter—un-numb the numbers.

> We had the *Encyclopedia Britannica* at home. When I was a small boy, [my father] used to sit me on his lap and read to me from the
>
> *Britannica.* We would be reading, say, about dinosaurs. It would be talking about the Tyrannosaurus rex, and it would say something like, "This dinosaur is twenty-five feet high and its head is six feet across."
>
> My father would stop reading and say, "Now, let's see what that means. That would mean that if he stood in our front yard, he would be tall enough to put his head through our window up here." (We were on the second floor.) "But his head would be too wide to fit in the window." Everything he read to me he would translate as best he could into some reality.

Assignment

Use the questions below to practice your own ability to un-numb the numbers.

1. "In the United States, per capita calories in a day rose from 2,100 calories in a day in 1970 to 2,568, according to the Department of Agriculture. That's equivalent to adding _____ to the daily diet of every American."

    —Michael Specter, "Freedom from Fries" (2015)

    A. two slices of bread
    B. two slices of Domino's Pizza
    C. two slices of tomato
    D. two slices of Velveeta cheese

2. "One of the reasons we find high dropout rates so puzzling is that dropping out is like throwing away a _____: the data tell us that for each year of school that a student misses, [their] earning power drops by roughly 12 percent. Indeed, the average annual income for a high school dropout in 2009 was $19,540, compared to $27,380 for a high school graduate. Multiply that number by twenty years, and you see an earnings differential of $156,800."

    —Uri Gneezy and John List, *The Why Axis: Hidden Motives and the Undiscovered Economics of Everyday Life* (2013)

    A. winning lottery ticket
    B. student loan
    C. credit report
    D. Treasury bond

3. "Facebook was one of four companies (along with Google, Amazon, and Apple) that dominated the Internet; the combined value of their stock is larger than the G.D.P. of
_____."

—Evan Osnos, "Can Mark Zuckerberg Fix Facebook before It Breaks Democracy?" (2018)

A. Fiji
B. Finland
C. France
D. Freedonia

Answer Key

1. **B. Two slices of Domino's Pizza.** The image of two pieces of cheesy Domino's Pizza would likely resonate with the audience of Specter's article, which was published in the *New Yorker*. That image is helpfully particular, caloric, and indulgent. Two of the other choices ("two slices of bread" and "two slices of tomato") are a bit too generic and healthy. The final option ("two slices of Velveeta cheese") is usefully specific, but it's not factually accurate. The calorie amount Specter is trying to translate is 468. That's a lot more than just two slices of Velveeta cheese, which would be more like 70 calories total.

2. **A. Winning lottery ticket.** Gneezy and List wanted to highlight the large financial reward that education brings. Referencing a winning lottery ticket is a great way to do that. The other choices ("student loan," "credit report," and "Treasury bond") all relate to finance, but none captures the windfall the way a winning lottery ticket does.

3. **C. France.** It is indeed true that the combined value of Facebook, Amazon, Apple, and Google was bigger than the GDP of each of the other countries when Osnos wrote his article. But France is the best choice because it is the richest country listed. That makes the comparison even more striking. (*Note:* Freedonia is the fictional country in the classic Marx Brothers movie *Duck Soup*.)

High-Stakes Project: Money, Time, Size

Numbers numb our feelings for what is being counted.
—Frederick Herzberg, quoted in *The Economist Guide
to Management Ideas and Gurus* (2012)

Background

Take a look at your high-stakes project. Are there any numbers in it
that might be good to un-numb or in some other way make more
meaningful and memorable?

Here are some categories to be particularly aware of, given how
frequently they come up in the professional world:

- Money
- Time
- Size

Assignment

You are about to see writers adroitly dealing with data and statistics
in the three categories mentioned above. Jot down some notes on the
strategies they use. What do they reach for as reference points? How
specific are their examples? Why do you think they constructed the
comparison they did?

Then try to incorporate similar strategies as you begin to un-numb
the numbers in your writing. Even if you are working on a very different kind of document than the books and articles in the examples,
there may still be compositional tactics you can productively borrow.
Expert editors and advocates draw on a wide range of sources.

Money

- "At the moment, the planet is on track to warm more than
  three degrees Celsius by century's end, which one recent

study found would do five hundred and fifty-one trillion dollars in damage. <u>That's more money than currently exists on the planet</u>."

> —Bill McKibben, "Money Is the Oxygen on Which
> the Fire of Global Warming Burns" (2019)

- "The total cost of the program [to eradicate smallpox—a disease that killed over 300 million people during the 20th century—] . . . was in the region of $312 million—perhaps 32 cents per person in infected countries. <u>The eradication program cost about the same as producing five recent Hollywood blockbusters, or the wing of a B-2 bomber, or a little under one-tenth the cost of Boston's recent road-improvement project nicknamed the Big Dig</u>. However much one admires the improved views of the Boston waterfront, the lines of the stealth bomber, or the acting skills of Keira Knightley in *Pirates of the Caribbean*, or indeed of the gorilla in *King Kong*, this [public health expenditure] still seems like a very good deal."

> —Charles Kenny, *Getting Better: Why Global
> Development Is Succeeding—and How We Can
> Improve the World Even More* (2011)

Time

- "Of the 3.5 trillion photos that have been snapped since the first image of a busy Parisian street in 1838, fully 10 percent were taken in the last year. Until recently, most photos were analog, created using silver halide and other chemicals. But analog photography peaked in 2000. Today, over 2.5 billion people have digital cameras and the vast majority of photos are digital. The effects are astonishing: <u>it has been estimated that more photos are now taken every two minutes than in all of the nineteenth century</u>."

—Erik Brynjolfsson and Andrew McAfee, *The Second Machine Age: Work, Progress, and Prosperity in a Time of Brilliant Technologies* (2014)

- "In like manner, geologists will sometimes use the calendar year as a unit to represent the time scale, and in such terms the Precambrian runs from New Year's Day until well after Halloween. Dinosaurs appear in the middle of December and are gone the day after Christmas. The last ice sheet melts on December 31st at one minute before midnight, and the Roman Empire lasts five seconds. <u>With your arms spread wide again to represent all time on earth, look at one hand with its line of life. The Cambrian begins in the wrist, and the Permian Extinction is at the outer end of the palm. All of the Cenozoic is in a fingerprint, and in a single stroke with a medium-grained nail file you could eradicate human history</u>."

—John McPhee, *Annals of the Former World* (1998)

Size

- "If an archer's aim is off by less than half a degree, she won't hit her target. 'Just moving your hand by one millimeter changes everything, especially when you're at the further distances,' said Sarah Chai, a recent Columbia graduate and former co-captain of the varsity archery team. From the standard seventy-five-yard distance from the target, <u>the bull's eye looks as small as a matchstick tip held out at arm's</u>

length. Hitting the eight-ring means piercing a circle the size of the hole in a bagel from 225 feet away."

—Sarah Lewis, *The Rise: Creativity, the Gift of Failure, and the Search for Mastery* (2014)

- "In the past sixty years, the population of Detroit has shrunk from two million to fewer than seven hundred thousand. Oakland County's population has followed the reverse trajectory. In 1960, its population was just under seven hundred thousand. About 1.2 million people live there now. If suburbs are parasites, this one is consuming its host. The county measures nine hundred and ten square miles, just shy of the size of Rhode Island."

—Paige Williams, "Drop Dead, Detroit!" (2014)

EPILOGUE

ELEPHANT IN THE ROOM

So will my page be colored that I write?

—Langston Hughes, "Theme for English B" (1951)

In the final weeks of the "Editing and Advocacy" course this book is based on, I have students do an exercise that often results in many of them sending me very thoughtful follow-up emails. You can try the exercise yourself. Simply list the titles of any books on writing you have read, heard of, or been assigned.

Perhaps, for example, your high school English teacher had you work through chapters of *The Elements of Style* by William Strunk and E. B. White. Or maybe a friend once recommended you check out *Eats, Shoots & Leaves* by Lynne Truss, the British grammarian who did something remarkable in 2004: she turned a book about punctuation into a *New York Times* bestseller.

Whatever your sources, whatever your educational background, the point of the exercise is to get a rough sense of who and what has shaped your understanding of what "good writing" is—particularly when it comes to the documents you're expected to produce in school or at work. The results may be illuminating.

In case your mental library is a bit bare at the moment, here's a collection of titles my students have offered during various terms. Seeing them might jog your memory:

- *Bird by Bird* by Anne Lamott
- *On Writing* by Stephen King
- *On Writing Well* by William Zinsser
- *Steering the Craft* by Ursula K. Le Guin
- *They Say / I Say* by Cathy Birkenstein and Gerald Graff
- *The Writing Life* by Annie Dillard
- *How to Write a Sentence* by Stanley Fish
- *Plain English for Lawyers* by Richard C. Wydick
- *Legal Writing in Plain English* by Bryan A. Garner
- *Point Made* by Ross Guberman
- *Drafting Contracts* by Tina L. Stark

Now comes the hard part: look at your list and try to find at least one author who *isn't* white. You don't have to find ten. You don't have to find five. You don't even have to find two. You only have to find one.

My guess is that this task will be depressingly difficult. It certainly has been for my students. One year, close to ninety people were in the class. Not one came up with a writing guide authored by a person of color. Nor did anyone in a separate seminar of twenty-five students a few days later. I think that's a problem.

A. Writing White

Over the past several decades, the student population at law schools across the country has become more and more racially diverse. In 1987, for example, only about one in every ten law students identified as a person of color. By 2019, that percentage shot up to almost one out of three.

Yet take a look at the list of books you put down (if you did the exercise)—or at virtually any set of recommended manuals on writing. The composition of law schools may be changing dramatically, but the materials that students and other advocates-in-training continue to be given to help them figure out how to put together documents that are proper, persuasive, and professional are designed pretty much exclusively by white people. "To write right," we seem to be saying, "you need to write white."

A student of mine identified this concern quite well in one of the follow-up emails I mentioned:

> As a student of color, I feel like there's always a towering elephant in the law school classroom: the overwhelming majority of case-book authors and professors are white. But no one talks about it, and they certainly don't talk about how this [homogeneity] controls the narrative.

Think of your own education. How many of your courses were taught by white professors? How many of your casebooks were written by white authors? Ninety percent? Ninety-five? One hundred?

Modupe Akinola, a professor at Columbia Business School, shared an anecdote on the podcast *Choiceology* that shows that this lack of diversity is certainly not limited to law schools. "I'd often find myself setting up to teach a class," she told the host of the podcast, behavioral scientist Katy Milkman, "and somebody, usually a prospective student, would come in and say, 'Oh, I'd like to sit in on this class and learn more about this class. Where's the professor?' Yes, they would say that to me, as I'm setting up, looking like the professor, on the computer getting everything ready."

Akinola then offers a couple of reasons why the "Where is the professor?" question keeps coming her way: "I look young, so yes, that's one of the reasons why they might ask. But I also am African American, and if you ask most people how many African American professors have you had, most would say zero or one. And then you ask them how many African American female professors have you had, and they would certainly say zero. Maybe some would say one."

B. White Forest, Dense Student

Akinola's story made me curious. How many African American female professors did I have when I was a student?* How about the number of professors of color in general?

Here's what a quick check of my transcripts revealed. In four years of college, five years of graduate school, and three years of law school,

---

* I recently followed the lead of many publications—including the *New York Times*—in using "Black" instead of "African American." But given that Akinola used "African American" when telling her anecdote, I decided to stick with that phrase as well. For an overview of how various style guides are navigating this issue, *see* Merrill Perlman, *AP Tackles Language about Race in This Year's Style Guide*, COLUM. JOURNALISM REV. (Apr. 1, 2019).

I had right around what Akinola predicted: a grand total of one African American female professor. But even that is a bit misleading. The "course" was a two-week trial advocacy workshop in law school that was team-taught by a bunch of professors. My senior faculty mentor in the workshop was white. So was my junior faculty mentor.

If we expand the category to include professors of color in general, the number increases a bit—but not by much. It drops to zero, however, if we focus on writing classes.

I take a lot of responsibility for that lack of curricular diversity. Professors of color existed at the law school I attended and at the universities where I went to college and graduate school. I could have done a much better job seeking out their courses. Even when I signed up for ones explicitly about race—"American Law and the Rhetoric of Race" in college; "Race, Radicalism, and the Cold War" and "African Americans and the Literary Left" in graduate school—they were taught by white people. Wonderful white people. Brilliant white people. But white people nonetheless.

I was too intellectually dense as a student to realize the consequences of these choices, and I was certainly too emotionally and culturally dense to realize something else: how hard it must have been for students of color to have to pick from that same disproportionately white menu of faculty. As Shaun Harper, the executive director of the USC Race and Equity Center, has noted, "If in every class, all your professors are white, it might signal to you that smart people of color don't belong here. Or when the only people who look like you are cutting the grass, emptying the trash, or frying French fries in the food court, that might suggest to you that my people are not thought of as professorial or professional."

When students build their schedules each semester, it can be tough for them to see how a set of decisions that seem individually reasonable can lead to a collectively undesirable result. I can't identify a specific course that I regret signing up for when I went through that process. I liked all the professors I picked. I now even consider many of them friends.

But when I take a more macro-level view of my transcripts and overall course selection, I definitely think to myself, "Man. Each individual tree was great, but the forest it created is regrettably white."

C. Rebalancing Your Portfolio

I share these regrets with my students so that they give some extra consideration to what kind of forests they want to create and inhabit—not just in their academic lives but also in their social lives, their political lives, and their professional lives. I also give them a short assignment, usually right after we do the "Elephant in the Room" exercise. The assignment builds off an earlier one called "Good Sentences," in which students are asked to devote thirty to sixty minutes each week to reading quality writing.

The "Good Sentences" assignment gives students a lot of control over what they decide to fill their brains with. One option is to choose from a mix of fiction, journalism, scholarly articles, briefs, and poetry related to whatever we are talking about in class that week. Maybe that's health law. Maybe that's intellectual property law. Maybe that's something like entrepreneurship or finance. A second option is to choose a book they've been meaning to start or finish.

The "Elephant in the Room" twist comes through the steps outlined below. I distribute them toward the end of the semester, after students have about eight to ten weeks of picking at least some of their own reading material.

Step 1: Think about the pieces you have picked to read during the "Good Sentences" assignments each week.

Step 2: Write down what you guess might be your personal breakdown in at least two of the categories below:

- *Genre:* Do you think you read more literary sentences than journalistic sentences? And if so, by how much? Did you read any poetic sentences? How about Supreme Court ones?

- *Gender:* Do you think you read more pieces by women than by men? More men than women? Did you read any pieces by someone who doesn't identify as a man or a woman?

- *Race/Ethnicity/Nationality:* This category might take some googling if you don't immediately recognize the authors.

- *Sexual Orientation:* This category also might take some googling.

- *Ideology:* Are you only reading conservative writers? Only liberal ones? One rough indicator may be the publications in which each piece was printed: *National Review* vs. *New Yorker* vs. *New York Times* vs. *Commentary.*

Step 3: After guessing what you thought your ratios might be, write down what your actual ratios were. Raw numbers can be instructive.

Step 4: Upload a paragraph of at least seventy-five words summarizing your findings from Steps 1–3. Include whether you want to make any changes to your current reading habits in the coming weeks, months, and years.

Does this assignment put more professors of color in the classroom? No. Does it miraculously even up the racial composition of casebook authors and style guides? Definitely not.

One thing it does do, however, is get students to think about how they might rebalance their intellectual portfolio. Here are some sample responses:

- "Gender is the factor I've been most aware of and have been trying to rebalance in my readings. Thinking back to the past 3 months, more than half of the political authors I have read were female, especially as I have become passionate about exploring more nuanced narratives on leadership and public service. Yet the clear lack of representation of non-binary individuals in my readings is a sign that I haven't done enough to seek out these authors. Especially among community organizers and advocates, there is much for me to explore and learn, and I want to commit to expanding the narratives I read."

- "I realize that despite my efforts to diversify my reading, the balance is still very white. I also realize that among the writers of color that I have read recently, almost all of them are Black. Very few are Latinx, Middle-Eastern, or Asian. I want to commit to expanding the narratives I read to include a wider range of racial and ethnic backgrounds. I know I still have a lot of work to do towards this goal."

- "This assignment has been both eye-opening and disturbing. I didn't realize how much of my life is dominated by white male influence. I don't think that this trend is by any means intentional, but it certainly seems like I unconsciously gravitate towards things penned and produced by white males. To get new perspectives, I will have to be intentional about reading things from different points of view and backgrounds."

- "In the last few years, I've made an intentional choice to try to read more work by queer women of color. Next year, I'd like to commit to reading more from authors who have a disability. I am going to be clerking for a judge with a significant physical disability after graduation, and it made me realize that I haven't done enough to center the perspective of people with disabilities in my own social circles or in my reading."

Much more than a new set of reading lists and habits is required to address the elephant in the room that my student rightly identified. But I am encouraged that there are ways—like the assignment this chapter describes—that can help people (myself in particular) become not just more aware of their mental inputs but genuinely committed to broadening them.

I am also encouraged that the student herself recently published a piece of legal scholarship, especially given that law reviews are another place that can be dispiritingly homogenous. Perhaps someday she'll even write an entire book or style guide. I'd love to add it to my syllabus.

ACKNOWLEDGMENTS

EDITING AND ADVOCACY
AND GRATITUDE

"Editing and Advocacy" is the name of the first course I ever created at the University of Michigan Law School. So it—and the fifty intrepid students who initially signed up for it—will always have a special place in my curricular heart.

Since then, I have had the wonderful experience of teaching versions of the course at the University of Chicago Law School and the UCLA School of Law. I am very grateful to the various deans, administrators, and internal champions who helped make that happen. It is great to be able to visit other institutions and not at all feel like an outsider.

I am also very grateful to the many students at both of those schools whose insightful comments inside and outside of class have dramatically improved the way I think about and communicate the concepts described in this book. Together with my students at Michigan, they have been the best editors and the most inspiring advocates I can imagine working with.

Finally, I would like to thank several journals and magazines who originally published portions of the book. Their skilled reviewers and staff always returned my drafts in better shape than when I submitted them.

ACKNOWLEDGMENTS

Chapters 1, 4, 8, and 9: *Michigan Bar Journal*

Chapter 2: *Journal of Legal Communication and Rhetoric*

Chapter 3: *Illinois Bar Journal*

Chapter 5: *Los Angeles Lawyer*

Chapter 6: *Journal of Appellate Practice*

Chapter 10 and Epilogue: *Scribes Journal of Legal Writing*

NOTES

Epigraph

viii **"Poetry is everywhere":** THE BEST AMERICAN POETRY 2013 198 (Denise Duhamel ed., 2013).

Introduction

xi **"every small refinement":** WILLIAM ZINSSER, ON WRITING WELL 87 (7th ed. 2006).

xiii **"Vehicles in the Park":** H. L. A. Hart, *Positivism and the Separation of Law and Morals*, 71 HARV. L. REV. 593, 607 (1958).

xiv **"one thing at a time":** BEN YAGODA, THE SOUND ON THE PAGE: GREAT WRITERS TALK ABOUT STYLE AND VOICE IN WRITING 199–200 (2004).

xv **"freewriting":** PETER ELBOW, WRITING WITHOUT TEACHERS 3–10 (2nd ed. 1998).

xv **"changeable":** Interview by Sharon Hamilton with M. H. Abrams (Mar. 10, 2007).

xv **"freeze at the first effort":** *Id.*

Teaching Style and Reading Tips

xviii **"learning a language for them":** Brooke Jarvis, *What Can COVID-19 Teach Us about the Mysteries of Smell?*, N.Y. TIMES MAGAZINE (Jan. 28, 2021).

xviii **"coproduced":** For a review of the benefits of educational coproduction, *see* Marlies Honingh, Elena Bondarouk & Taco Brandsen, *Co-production* *in Primary Schools: A Systematic Literature Review*, 86(2) Int'l Rev. of Admin. Sci. 222–39 (2020).

xix **"require one to attain more in order to be satisfied"**: Edwin A. Locke & Gary P. Latham, *New Directions in Goal-Setting Theory*, 15(5) Current Directions in Psych. Sci. 265 (2006).

xix **"vague goals"**: *Id.*

Part I

1 **"success consists"**: Italo Calvino, Six Memos for the Next Millennium 48–49 (Patrick Creigh trans., 1988).

Chapter 1

3 **"exercise in empathy"**: Samantha Power, *Samantha Power to Grads: Start Changing the World by "Acting as If,"* Time (May 18, 2015).

4 **"empathy is a cornerstone of design"**: *Abstract: The Art of Design: Ilse Crawford: Interior Design* (Netflix broadcast, Feb. 10, 2017).

5 **"focus group"**: *See, e.g.,* David Lat, *Supreme Court Clerk Hiring Watch: To Know a Judge, Know Her Clerks*, Above the Law (July 19, 2017, 6:28 P.M.), https://abovethelaw.com/2017/07/supreme-court-clerk -hiring-watch-to-know-a-judge-know-her-clerks/.

6 **"George Saunders has become a kind of superhero"**: Joel Lovell, *George Saunders Has Written the Best Book You'll Read All Year*, N.Y. Times (Jan. 3, 2013).

6 **"humane, bright, witty, experienced, and well-intentioned as you"**: George Saunders, *What Writers Really Do When They Write*, Guardian (Mar. 4, 2017). I thank Marcos Kotlik, a wonderfully learned and intellectually curious Michigan Law alum from Argentina, for putting Saunders's essay on my radar.

6 **"welcome [them] in"**: *Id.*

7 **"judicial opinion on a silver platter"**: University of Chicago Law School, *Justice Ruth Bader Ginsburg and Geoffrey Stone, "Rowe at 40,"* YouTube (Jun. 5, 2013), https://www.youtube.com/watch?v=xw3CMRyvkq4&t=49s.

7 **"convert into an opinion"**: *Id.*

8 **"paradigm-shifting protections"**: *Craig v. Boren*, 429 U.S. 190 (1976); *Frontiero v. Richardson*, 411 U.S. 677 (1973); *Reed v. Reed*, 404 U.S. 71 (1971).

8   **"the Thurgood Marshall of [women's rights]"**: Antonin Scalia, *Ruth Bader Ginsburg: The High Court's Counterweight*, TIME (Apr. 16, 2015), https://time.com/collection-post/3823889/ruth-bader-ginsburg-2015 -time-100/.

9   **"the advocate is angling"**: John W. Davis, *The Argument of an Appeal*, 26 A. B. A. J. 895, 895 (1940).

9   **"ideas to people and people to ideas"**: Donald C. Bryant, *Rhetoric: Its Function and Its Scope*, 39 Q. J. OF SPEECH 401 (Dec. 1953).

10 **"the right word, and the right word order"**: Ruth Bader Ginsburg, *Ruth Bader Ginsburg's Advice for Living*, N.Y. TIMES (Oct. 2, 2016).

10 **"as spare as I could"**: Bryan A. Garner, *Interviews with United States Supreme Court Justices*, 13 SCRIBES J. OF LEGAL WRITING 1, 135 (2010).

12 **"leaner version"**: JANE SHERRON DE HART, RUTH BADER GINSBURG: A LIFE 129 (2016).

14 **"no idea"**: BO SEO, GOOD ARGUMENTS 276 (2022).

14 **"paid to read our writing"**: Larry McEnerney & UChicago Social Sciences, *Leadership Lab: The Craft of Writing Effectively*, YOUTUBE (Jun. 26, 2014), https://www.youtube.com/watch?v=vtIzMaLkCaM.

14 **"switch to something else"**: Farhad Manjoo, *You Won't Finish This Article*, SLATE (Jun. 6, 2013, 7:03 P.M.).

Chapter 2

17 **"space out practice"**: PETER BROWN, HENRY ROEDIGER & MARK MCDANIEL, MAKE IT STICK: THE SCIENCE OF SUCCESSFUL LEARNING 4 (2014).

18 **"Journal articles promote interleaving"**: *See, e.g.*, Jennifer M. Cooper & Regan A. R. Gurung, *Smarter Law Study Habits: An Empirical Analysis of Law Learning Strategies and Relationship with Law GPA*, 62 ST. LOUIS U. L. J. 361, 373 (2017); Jennifer M. Cooper, *Smarter Law Learning: Using Cognitive Science to Maximize Law Learning*, 44 CAP. U. L. REV. 551, 570–72 (2016).

18 **"Popular websites promote interleaving"**: *See, e.g.*, Matt Shinners, *Master the LSAT with Learning Science*, ABOVE THE LAW (Apr. 13, 2017, 11:34 A.M.), https://abovethelaw.com/2017/04/master-the-lsat-with-learning-science/ ?rf=1; *More Memory Advice for the Bar Exam*, LAW PROFESSOR BLOGS (Jun. 17, 2020), https://lawprofessors.typepad.com/academic_support/ 2020/06/more-memory-advice-for-the-bar-exam.html.

18 **"university research centers"**: *See, e.g.*, *Supporting Student Learning and Performance*, University of Michigan Center for Research on Learning and Teaching (2022), https://crlt.umich.edu/olws/6/supporting; *Reading Analytically for Social Science*, Yale Poorvu Center for Teaching and Learning (2022), https://poorvucenter.yale.edu/sites/default/files/basic-page-supplementary-materials-files/stratgies_for_online_exams.pptx.

18 **"an effective strategy is to interleave"**: *Research*, UCLA Bjork Learning & Forgetting Lab, https://bjorklab.psych.ucla.edu/research/.

18 **"desirable difficulties"**: Elizabeth L. Bjork & Robert Bjork, *Making Things Hard on Yourself, but in a Good Way: Creating Desirable Difficulties to Enhance Learning*, in Psychology and the Real World: Essays Illustrating Fundamental Contributions to Society 56 (Morton Ann Gernsbacher et al. eds., 2009).

18 **"deeper and longer-lasting comprehension"**: *See, e.g.*, Robert Bjork & Judith Kroll, *Desirable Difficulties in Vocabulary Learning*, 128 Am. J. Psychol. 241, 245–47 (2015); Henry Roediger & Kathleen McDermott, *Remembering What We Learn*, Cerebrum (July 19, 2018).

18 **"spacing"**: *See, e.g.*, Harry P. Bahrick et al., *Maintenance of Foreign Language Vocabulary and the Spacing Effect*, 4 Psychol. Sci. 316, 316–21 (1993); Michael J. Kahana & Marc W. Howard, *Spacing and Lag Effects in Free Recall of Pure Lists*, 12 Psychonomic Bull. & Rev. 159–64 (2005); John J. Shaughnessy, *Long-Term Retention and the Spacing Effect in Free-Recall and Frequency Judgments*, 90 Am. J. Psychol. 587–98 (1977).

19 **"neural pathways"**: *See, e.g.*, Haley A. Vlach & Catherine M. Sandhofer, *Distributing Learning over Time: The Spacing Effect in Children's Acquisition and Generalization of Science Concepts*, 83 Child Dev. 1137 (2012); Robert Bjork, *Memory and Meta-memory Considerations in the Training of Human Beings*, in Metacognition: Knowing about Knowing 185 (Arthur Shimamura & Janet Metcalfe eds., 1994).

19 **"more retrievable in the future"**: Garth Sundem, *Everything You Thought You Knew about Learning Is Wrong*, Wired (Jan. 29, 2012).

19 **"flash cards"**: R. Schmidmaier, R. Ebersbach, M. Schiller, I. Hege, M. Holzer & M. R. Fischer, *Using Electronic Flashcards to Promote Learning in Medical Students: Retesting versus Restudying*, 45 Medical Education 1101–10 (2011); J. M. Golding, N. E. Wasarhaley & B. Fletcher, *The Use*

of Flashcards in an Introduction to Psychology Class, 39 Teaching of Psychology 199–202 (2012).

19   **"Jeffrey Fisher"**: To read more about Jeffrey Fisher, *see Jeffrey L. Fisher: Biography*, Stan. L. Sch., https://law.stanford.edu/directory/jeffrey-l-fisher/#slsnav-featured-video.

20   **"greater harvest"**: *See* Rachel Toor, *The Habits of Highly Productive Writers*, Chron. Higher Educ. (Nov. 17, 2014).

20   **"the work has been done while one slept or shopped or talked with friends"**: *Id.* (quoting Graham Greene, The End of the Affair 19 [1951]).

20   **"THE POET IS WORKING"**: André Breton, *Manifesto of Surrealism (1924)*, 391 Issues, http://391.org/manifestos/1924-manifesto-of-surrealism-andre-breton/.

20   **"resolved in the morning"**: John Steinbeck, Sweet Thursday 107 (1954). For more on how your "resting" brain is really quite an active and productive brain, *see* Deirdre Barrett, The Committee of Sleep: How Artists, Scientists, and Athletes Use Dreams for Creative Problem-Solving and How You Can Too (2001); Mary Helen Immordino-Yang et al., *Rest Is Not Idleness: Implications of the Brain's Default Mode for Human Development and Education*, 7 Perspectives on Psych. Sci. 352 (Jun. 29, 2012).

21   **"blocking"**: For more on the difference between "blocking" and "interleaving" strategies, *see* Paulo Carvalho & Robert Goldstone, *Effects of Interleaved and Blocked Study on Delayed Test of Category of Learning Generalization*, 5 Frontiers Psychol. 936 (2014).

21   **"related set of benefits"**: Adam Grant, *Why I Taught Myself to Procrastinate*, N.Y. Times: Opinion (Jan. 16, 2016).

21   **"two years in advance"**: Adam Grant, *Why I Taught Myself to Procrastinate*, N.Y. Times: Opinion (Jan. 16, 2016).

21   **"worth doing early"**: *Id.*

21   **"perspective changed"**: *Id.*

22   **"boost in creative thinking"**: Jihae Shin & Adam M. Grant, *When Putting Work Off Pays Off: The Curvilinear Relationship between Procrastination and Creativity*, Acad. of Mgmt. J. (Apr. 3, 2020).

22   **"between when you start and when you finish"**: In a critique of Grant's essay, the psychologist Tim Pychyl distinguishes between "delay" and "procrastination": "[Grant's] notion of 'the right kind of procrastination . . .' is

the thesis and main error of the essay. The right kind of *delay* may make you more creative. I agree that being too quick off the mark for all of your tasks may be an ineffective strategy when careful thought is necessary first. But, please, let's not play in this semantic cesspool. All delay is not procrastination, and it's important to know the difference. When you figure that out, you'll probably use delay more effectively, and you'll probably be more creative." Tim Pychyl, *Procrastination as a Virtue for Creativity: Why It's False*, PSYCHOL. TODAY (Jan. 18, 2016). For an additional critique, *see* Piers Steel, *The Original Myth*, PSYCHOL. TODAY (Apr. 8, 2016).

22　**"spotting unexpected patterns"**: Adam Grant, *Why I Taught Myself to Procrastinate*, N.Y. TIMES: OPINION (Jan. 16, 2016).

22　**"fresh material at my disposal"**: *Id.*

22　**"more creative and discerning compositional lens"**: For other endorsements of this kind of spacing, *see* Tonya Kowalski, *Toward a Pedagogy for Teaching Legal Writing in Law School Clinics*, 17 CLINICAL L. REV. 285, 338 (2011) ("It is not realistic to expect students to have strong time management skills when it comes to producing new types of work product because they simply do not yet have the experience to fully comprehend what is expected or entailed. Professors can scaffold students into this understanding by requiring modular drafts and deadlines at first, and then increasingly leaving it up to the more self-directed students to set their own drafting schedules as the semester goes on."); Terry Jean Seligmann, *Why Is a Legal Memorandum like an Onion? A Student's Guide to Reviewing and Editing*, 56 MERCER L. REV. 729, 731–32 (2005) ("One could, in theory, read the memorandum several times, each time focusing on a different level of review. In practice, as with the onion, both the writer and reader will look at the layers at the same time as a whole. By focusing on these levels as a separable series of critiques, you can assure that you have considered the range of editorial issues that your legal memorandum raises."); Christopher M. Anzidei, *The Revision Process in Legal Writing: Seeing Better to Write Better*, 8 LEGAL WRITING 23, 30 (2002) ("A recursive model of the writing process suggests that writers constantly move back and forth to redo or repeat various composing activities as they progress toward project completion. The idea behind recursion is that when writers move back and forth in their text, they 'tear down' much of what they have written, and then rebuild their text, making it even stronger.").

23 **"go back and forth":** Noah Charney, *Cass Sunstein: How I Write*, DAILY BEAST (April 17, 2013).

23 **"not good at doing two things simultaneously":** *See, e.g.*, Melina R. Uncapher & Anthony D. Wagner, *Minds and Brains of Media Multitaskers: Current Findings and Future Directions*, 115 PROC. NAT'L ACAD. SCI. 9889 (Oct. 2, 2018).

24 **"seven different things":** Jonah Weiner, *Seth Rogen and the Secret to Happiness*, N.Y. TIMES (Apr. 20, 2021). Rogen adds a helpful caveat to his statement about the number of projects he works on every day: "But I don't have kids!"

24 **"She worked six days a week, and dreaded Sundays and holidays":** MASON CURREY, DAILY RITUALS: WOMEN AT WORK 31 (2019).

24 **"one project to another":** Noah Charney, *Cass Sunstein: How I Write*, DAILY BEAST (April 17, 2013).

25 **"The repetition itself becomes the important thing":** John Wray, *Haruki Murakami, the Art of Fiction No. 182*, PARIS REV. (Summer 2004).

26 **"peaceful, invigorating environments":** PAUL ZALLO, SONGWRITERS ON SONGWRITING 69 (Da Capo Press 2003) (1991).

26 **"I do best when I divide my attention":** *An Interview with Sandra Faber*, ANNUAL REVIEWS AUDIO (Dec. 7, 2009) (transcript available at https://www.annualreviews.org/userimages/ContentEditor/1299600853298/SandraFaberInterviewTranscript.pdf).

28 **"spare thoughts to literature":** *The Project Gutenberg EBook of Letters of Anton Chekhov, by Anton Chekhov*, PROJECT GUTENBERG (Dec. 8, 2002).

28 **"the energy of two men":** WILLIAM CARLOS WILLIAMS, THE AUTOBIOGRAPHY OF WILLIAM CARLOS WILLIAMS 359 (1967).

28 **"neither of them loses anything through my infidelity":** Letter from Anton Chekhov to A. S. Surovin (Sept. 11, 1888).

29 **"part of our attention":** Sophie Leroy, *Attention Residue*, UNIVERSITY OF WASHINGTON BOTHELL; *see also* Sophie Leroy, *Why Is It So Hard to Do My Work? The Challenges of Attention Residue When Switching between Work Tasks*, 109 ORG. BEH. & HUM. DECISION PROCESS 168 (July 2009).

29 **"produced ideas that were both more novel and more flexible":** Jackson Lu et al., *"Switching On" Creativity: Task Switching Can Increase Creativity by Reducing Cognitive Fixation*, 139 ORG. BEH. & HUM. DECISION PROCESS 63 (Mar. 2017).

30 **"cognitive fixation":** *Id.*

30 **"other studies"**: *See, e.g.,* Benjamin Baird et al., *Inspired by Distraction: Mind Wandering Facilitates Creative Incubation,* 23 PSYCH. SCI. 1117 (Aug. 31, 2012); Ut Na Sio & Thomas C. Ormerod, *Does Incubation Enhance Problem Solving? A Meta-analytic Review,* 135 PSYCH. BULL. 94 (Jan. 2009); Ap Dijksterhuis & Teun Meurs, *Where Creativity Resides: The Generative Power of Unconscious Thought,* 15 CONSCIOUSNESS & COGNITION 135 (Mar. 2006). Summarizing these studies, the Columbia team notes the common theme "is that setting a task aside may reduce cognitive fixation and enable individuals to approach the focal task with a fresh mind, thereby enhancing creative performance." Jackson Lu et al., *"Switching On" Creativity: Task Switching Can Increase Creativity by Reducing Cognitive Fixation,* 139 ORG. BEH. & HUM. DECISION PROCESS 63 (Mar. 2017).

Part II

33 **"I play with words"**: DORIS LESSING, THE GOLDEN NOTEBOOK 592 (1994).

35 **"find, sort, and activate that knowledge"**: For a good overview of how the retrieval process creates learning, *see* Jeffrey D. Karpicke, *A Powerful Way to Improve Learning and Memory,* PSYCHOL. SCI. AGENDA (Jun. 2016).

Chapter 3

39 **"better for your career if you fix your own mistakes"**: MARK HERRMANN, THE CURMUDGEON'S GUIDE TO PRACTICING LAW 3 (2006).

44 **"Acknowledgments"**: For an interesting look at what can be gleaned from the "Acknowledgments" section in law review articles, *see* Jonathan I. Tietz & W. Nicholson Price II, *Acknowledgments as a Window into Legal Academia,* 98 WASH. U. L. REV. 307 (2020). Works of fiction don't typically come with an "Acknowledgments" section. But fortunately, many authors create the spoken equivalent in interviews and acceptance speeches by thanking the various editors, cheerleaders, and initial readers who helped their books come into being.

44 **"finished from her pen"**: *Manuscripts Suggest Jane Austen Had a Great Editor,* NPR (Oct. 27, 2010).

45 **"recent archival research"**: Jennifer Howard, *Jane Austen's Well-Known Style Owed Much to Her Editor, Scholar Argues,* CHRON. HIGHER EDUC. (Oct. 22, 2010).

45 **"an unbreakable mandate"**: For a helpful set of questions you can ask when deciding whether to follow a certain grammar prohibition, *see* Steven Pinker, *Steven Pinker: 10 "Grammar Rules" It's OK to Break (Sometimes)*, GUARDIAN (Aug. 15, 2014). Here are a few: "Has the rule been respected by the best writers in the past? Is it respected by careful writers in the present? Is there a consensus among discerning writers that it conveys an interesting semantic distinction? And are violations of the rule obvious products of mishearing, careless reading, or a chintzy attempt to sound highfalutin?" Perhaps the most important, however, is the following one: "Do attempts to fix a sentence so that it obeys the rule only make it clumsier and less clear?"

47 **"pet peeves worth appreciating"**: Janet Maslin, HOW TO WRITE (IF YOU'RE STEPHEN KING), N.Y. TIMES (OCT. 5, 2000)

47 **"surveyed over one thousand state and federal judges"**: Ross Guberman, *Speaking Softly*, LITIGATION (Jun. 1, 2018).

49 **"annual conference for the Society for Editing"**: Emmy Favilla, *30 Copy Editors Tell Us Their Pet Peeves*, BUZZFEED.COM (Nov. 2, 2017), https://www.buzzfeed.com/emmyf/impact-as-a-verb-is-totally-fine.

49 **"Council of Science Editors"**: Jennifer Ann Hutt, *Science Editors and Their Pet Peeves*, 26 SCIENCE EDITOR 124–25 (2003), https://www.councilscienceeditors.org/wp-content/uploads/v26n4p124-125.pdf.

50 **"undying gratitude"**: *Id.* at 125.

51 **"channeled something more essential"**: BARACK OBAMA, A PROMISED LAND 358 (2020).

52 **"live with those every day"**: Rebecca Keegan, *In "Lincoln's" Beginning Was the Word*, L. A. TIMES (Nov. 15, 2012).

52 **"Leonardo DiCaprio"**: Clarisse Loughrey, *Jordan Belfort Had to Teach Leonardo DiCaprio How to Look like He Was on Drugs for the World of Wall Street*, INDEPENDENT (Sept. 18, 2017).

Chapter 4

55 **"more intelligent in the morning"**: Toni Morrison, *The Art of Fiction No. 134*, PARIS REV. (Fall 1993).

56 **"All animals are equal"**: GEORGE ORWELL, ANIMAL FARM 77 (Signet 2004) (1945).

56 **"allowed to operate"**: MATTHEW WALKER, WHY WE SLEEP: UNLOCKING THE POWER OF SLEEP AND DREAMS 13–14 (2017). In Walker's view, "a

societal change is needed, offering accommodations not dissimilar to those we make for other physically determined differences (e.g. sight impaired). We require supple work schedules that better adapt to both morning larks and night owls, and not just one in its extreme."

57 **"any other hour of the day"**: *Michael Chabon Q&A: Fatherhood and Writing at Midnight*, L. A. TIMES (Oct. 13, 2009).

57 **"similarly nocturnal approach"**: Caleb Melby & Heather Perlberg, *Nobody Makes Money like Apollo's Ruthless Founder Leon Black*, BLOOMBERG BUSINESSWEEK (Jan. 16, 2020): "Black's night-owl tendencies made him well-suited to handling one of Drexel's most important clients, Carl Icahn, who preferred doing business past midnight."

57 **"make space for vulnerability and the possibility of failure"**: AMY WHITAKER, ART THINKING: HOW TO CARVE OUT CREATIVE SPACE IN A WORLD OF SCHEDULES, BUDGETS, AND BOSSES 5 (2016).

58 **"ritualized time"**: Rebecca Knight, *MBA-Toting Evangelist for "Art Thinking" at Work*, FIN. TIMES (July 3, 2019).

58 **"deep work"**: CAL NEWPORT, DEEP WORK: RULES FOR FOCUSED SUCCESS IN A DISTRACTED WORLD 3 (2016).

58 **"shallow work"**: *Id.* at 6.

60 **"acquainted with the night"**: Robert Frost, *Acquainted with the Night*, 4 VA. Q. REV. 4 (1928).

60 **"every morning"**: Ernest Hemingway, *The Art of Fiction No. 21*, PARIS REV. (Spring 1958).

60 **"work until one"**: Simone de Beauvoir, *The Art of Fiction No. 35*, PARIS REV. (Spring–Summer 1965).

60 **"No intrusions"**: HENRY MILLER, HENRY MILLER ON WRITING 162 (1964).

61 **"Robert Frost was up late"**: Matt Shoard, *Writing at Night*, GUARDIAN (Dec. 21, 2010).

61 **"psychologist Alison Gopnik"**: HELEN SWORD, AIR & LIGHT & TIME & SPACE: HOW SUCCESSFUL ACADEMICS WRITE 21 (2017).

61 **"physicist Sun Kwok"**: Helen Sword, *"Write Every Day!" A Mantra Dismantled*, 21 INT'L J. FOR ACAD. DEV. 312, 318 (2016).

61 **"silver lining of fatigue"**: LEONARD MLODINOW, ELASTIC: UNLOCKING YOUR BRAIN'S ABILITY TO EMBRACE CHANGE 208 (2018).

62 **"burnt out"**: *Id.* at 209–10.

62 **"foggy and otherwise useless morning time"**: *Id.* at 210.

62 **"listen to my rhythms"**: *Id.*

63 **"meeting today is 'no Paris'"**: Donna Flynn, *Managing a Team across 5 Time Zones*, Harv. Bus. Rev. (Jun. 17, 2014).

Part III

65 **"you can revise"**: Bernard Malamud, The Tenants 183 (1971).

67 **"learning and retention"**: Ruth Helyer, *Learning through Reflection: The Critical Role of Reflection in Work-Based Learning (WBL)*, 7 J. of Work-Applied Mgmt. 15–27 (2015); Magdeleine D. N. Lew & Henk G. Schmidt, *Self-Reflection and Academic Performance: Is There a Relationship?*, 16 Advances in Health Sci. Educ. Theory and Prac. 529–545 (2011); Brikena Xhaferi & Gezim Xhaferi, *Enhancing Learning through Reflection—a Case Study of SEEU*, 12 SEEU Rev. 53–68 (2017).

67 **"asking yourself questions"**: Olga Khazan, *How to Learn New Things as an Adult*, Atlantic (Mar. 16, 2017).

Chapter 5

71 **"useful forms"**: Nathan Heller, *The Philosopher Redefining Equality*, New Yorker (Dec. 31, 2018).

72 **"food drive on a college campus"**: Chip Heath & Dan Heath, Switch: How to Change Things When Change Is Hard 182–83 (2010).

72 **"Better instructions"**: For an extended discussion about the "navigability" of documents, especially those produced by the government, *see* Cass R. Sunstein, Simpler: The Future of Government (2013).

73 **"jerk with a map"**: Chip Heath & Dan Heath, Switch: How to Change Things When Change Is Hard 183 (2010).

75 **"map of an abstract conceptual space"**: Hannah Fry, *Maps without Places*, New Yorker (Jun. 21, 2021) at 64.

75 **"hobbies"**: Andrew Marantz, *Jack Antonoff's Gift for Pop-Music Collaboration*, New Yorker (May 16, 2022), https://www.newyorker.com/magazine/2022/05/23/jack-antonoff-pop-music-collaboration-lorde-taylor-swift.

75 **"carve a new path"**: Rebecca Solnit, Wanderlust: A History of Walking 72 (2000).

75 **"take readers by the hand"**: Marc Tracy, *"The Free World" Explains How Culture Heated Up during the Cold War*, N.Y. Times (Apr. 18, 2021).

77 **"clear signals"**: *Reverse Outlining*, Amherst Coll. Writing Ctr., https://www.amherst.edu/academiclife/support/writingcenter/ resourcesforwriters/revision/reverse_outline.

77 **"Reverse outlining"**: *Id.*

Chapter 6

79 **"Sentences come in three forms"**: Jacques Barzun, Simple and Direct: A Rhetoric for Writers 189 (4th ed. 2001) (1975).

81 **"simple sentence"**: Eds. of Merriam-Webster's Collegiate Dictionary, Merriam-Webster's Manual for Writers & Editors: A Clear, Authoritative Guide to Effective Writing and Publishing 380 (1998).

81 **"page of history"**: *New York Trust Co. v. Eisner*, 256 U.S. 345, 349 (1921).

81 **"fire in a theatre"**: *Schenck v. United States*, 249 U.S. 47, 52 (1919).

81 **"does not enact"**: *Lochner v. New York*, 198 U.S. 45, 75 (1905) (Holmes, J., dissenting).

81 **"compound sentence"**: Eds. of Merriam-Webster's Collegiate Dictionary, Merriam-Webster's Manual for Writers & Editors: A Clear, Authoritative Guide to Effective Writing and Publishing 380 (1998).

82 **"Even a dog"**: Oliver Wendell Holmes Jr., The Common Law 3 (1881).

82 **"clavicle in"**: Oliver Wendell Holmes Jr., *Common Carriers and the Common Law*, 13 Am. L. Rev. 609, 630 (1879).

82 **"book of mathematics"**: Oliver Wendell Holmes Jr., The Common Law 3 (1881).

82 **"a bad man"**: Oliver Wendell Holmes Jr., *The Path of the Law*, 10 Harv. L. Rev. 457, 459 (1897).

82 **"complex sentence"**: Eds. of Merriam-Webster's Collegiate Dictionary, Merriam-Webster's Manual for Writers & Editors: A Clear, Authoritative Guide to Effective Writing and Publishing 380 (1998).

83 **"eternally vigilant"**: *Abrams v. United States*, 250 U.S. 616, 630 (1919) (Holmes, J., dissenting).

83 "Three generations of imbeciles": *Buck v. Bell*, 274 U.S. 200, 207 (1927).

83 "imagined future majority": Oliver Wendell Holmes Jr., *Natural Law*, 32 HARV. L. REV. 40 (1918).

85 "treated as criminals": THOMAS HEALY, THE GREAT DISSENT: HOW OLIVER WENDELL HOLMES CHANGED HIS MIND—AND CHANGED THE HISTORY OF FREE SPEECH IN AMERICA 2 (2013).

86 "making sentences": VERLYN KLINKENBORG, SEVERAL SHORT SENTENCES ABOUT WRITING 13 (2012).

Part IV

89 "retyping Hemingway's sentences": Nathan Heller, *The Falconer*, NEW YORKER (Jan. 25, 2021).

93 "has to be worked for": JACQUES BARZUN, TEACHER IN AMERICA 48 (1945).

93 "continued to write": Edward Rothstein, *Jacques Barzun Dies at 104; Cultural Critic Saw the Sun Setting on the West*, N.Y. TIMES (Oct. 25, 2012).

Chapter 7

95 "simple declarative sentence": ROBERT FROST, A GOOD PLACE TO START: THE LETTERS OF ROBERT FROST: VOLUME I 1886–1920 122–23 (Donald Sheehy, Mark Richardson & Robert Faggen eds., 2014) (quoting Frost's July 4, 1913, letter to John Bartlett).

96 "sound *dumber*, not smarter": NOAH A. MESSING, THE ART OF ADVOCACY: BRIEFS, MOTIONS, AND WRITING STRATEGIES OF AMERICA'S BEST LAWYERS 247 (2013); *see also* Daniel M. Oppenheimer, *Consequences of Erudite Vernacular Utilized Irrespective of Necessity: Problems with Using Long Words Needlessly*, 20 APPL. COGNITIVE PSYCHOL. 139 (2006) (summarizing empirical studies).

96 "easier for them to edit": NOAH A. MESSING, THE ART OF ADVOCACY: BRIEFS, MOTIONS, AND WRITING STRATEGIES OF AMERICA'S BEST LAWYERS 247 (2013).

96 "grow dull": *Id.* at 249.

97 "Variety makes them more effective": *See generally* Mark Finchman & John O'Brien, *Three Point Shooting and Efficient Mixed Strategies: A Portfolio Management Approach*, 4 J. SPORTS ANALYTICS 107 (2018) (applying theory underlying risk management in competitive financial markets to professional basketball games).

97 **"soccer prodigy"**: David Foster Wallace, *Roger Federer as Religious Experience*, N.Y. TIMES (Aug. 20, 2006).

98 **"style guides"**: *See, e.g.*, BRYAN A. GARNER, LEGAL WRITING IN PLAIN ENGLISH: A TEXT WITH EXERCISES 27 (2013); JOSEPH KIMBLE, LIFTING THE FOG OF LEGALESE 71 (2006); MARTIN CUTTS, OXFORD GUIDE TO PLAIN ENGLISH 1 (4th ed. 2013).

98 **"middle octave"**: JOSEPH M. WILLIAMS, STYLE: TOWARD CLARITY AND GRACE 135 (1990).

99 **"greatest adornment"**: Pico Iyer, *In Praise of the Humble Comma*, TIME (Jan. 24, 2001).

99 **"lost to us"**: *Id.*

99 **"bumper sticker"**: *Id.*

99 **"vital and alive"**: C. Robert Jennings, *Dr. Seuss: "What Am I Doing Here?,"* SAT. EVENING POST (Oct. 23, 1965).

99 **"catch their breath"**: BEN YAGODA, THE SOUND ON THE PAGE: GREAT WRITERS TALK ABOUT STYLE AND VOICE IN WRITING 44 (2004).

100 **"guaranteed money"**: DAVID HALBERSTAM, THE BREAKS OF THE GAME 5 (1981).

101 **"I am an invisible man"**: RALPH ELLISON, INVISIBLE MAN 1 (1952).

101 **"jazzlike"**: For a closer look at the role jazz plays in Ralph Ellison's writing, *see* Andrew Radford, *Ralph Ellison and Improvised History*, 52 MIDWEST Q. (Winter 2011). For a collection of Ellison's own essays on jazz, *see* RALPH ELLISON, LIVING WITH MUSIC: RALPH ELLISON'S JAZZ WRITINGS (Robert G. O'Meally ed., Modern Library Classics ed. 2002) (2001).

101 **"planned to be a classical composer"**: ARNOLD RAMPERSAD, RALPH ELLISON: A BIOGRAPHY 41–49 (2008).

102 **"Call me Ishmael"**: HERMAN MELVILLE, MOBY DICK 1 (1851). The range here is eighty-four words.

102 **"I'm pretty much fucked"**: ANDY WEIR, THE MARTIAN 1 (2014). The range here is twenty-four words.

103 **"offense was blackness"**: DOUGLAS BLACKMON, SLAVERY BY ANOTHER NAME 1 (2008).

104 **"Professor John Pottow, used this technique"**: For a more extended discussion of Professor Pottow's use of short and long sentences in that brief, *see* Patrick Barry, *Shot Selection*, 19 J. APP. PRAC. & PROCESS 157 (2018). The "Shot Selection" chapter in this book is adapted from that article.

105 **"Not so"**: Defendants Wei Seng Phua and Darren Wai Kit Phua's Joint Objection to Magistrate Judge Leen's Report and Recommendation (DKT #407) at 4, *US v. Phua*, 100 F. Supp. 3d 1040 (D. Nev. Feb. 17, 2015) (No. 2:14-CR-00249-APG-PAL).

105 **"prosecutor's main arguments"**: Soccer fans and sports gamblers may remember the case because Mr. Goldstein's client, Paul Phua, was perhaps the world's biggest sports bookie at the time. Disclosure: I remember the case because I worked on it as a law clerk for Judge Andrew P. Gordon of the US District Court in Las Vegas.

105 **"sharp nails"**: *See, e.g.*, Tryon Edwards, A Dictionary of Thoughts: Being a Cyclopedia of Laconic Quotations 338 (1891) (attributing maxim to Diderot).

106 **"fluctuated your expectations"**: David Bianculli, The Platinum Age of Television 236 (2016).

106 **"rhythm of your sentences"**: Teju Cole, *Words Follow Me*, Next (Oct. 27, 2010).

107 **"Everyone complains that lawyers' sentences are too long"**: Ross Guberman, Point Made: How to Write like the Nation's Top Advocates 227 (2010).

107 **"Punctuation is the music of language"**: Noah Lukeman, A Dash of Style: The Art and Mastery of Punctuation 14 (2007).

111 **"An assumption exists"**: Brooks Landon, Building Great Sentences: Exploring the Writer's Craft 84 (2008).

Chapter 8

113 **"style of paragraphing"**: Edward P. J. Corbett, Classical Rhetoric for the Modern Student 440 (1971).

114 **"every preceding paragraph"**: Andy Bodle, *Breaking Point: Is the Writing on the Wall for the Paragraph?*, Guardian (May 22, 2015).

115 **"visually monotonous text"**: Steven Pinker, The Sense of Style: The Thinking Person's Guide to Writing in the 21st Century 145 (2014).

116 **"The facts of the crime"**: Brief for Petitioner-Appellant at 3, *Makowski v. Snyder*, 495 Mich 465; 852 NW2d 61 (2014) (No. 146867).

121 **"Inhale at the beginning of the paragraph"**: Francine Prose, Reading Like a Writer 66 (2006).

121 **"obituary"**: *Philip Roth Was One of America's Greatest Novelists*, ECONO-MIST (May 26, 2018).

123 **"husbands again"**: PHILIP ROTH, AMERICAN PASTORAL 3–4 (1997).

123 **"I am Philip Roth"**: Philip Roth, *An Open Letter to Wikipedia*, NEW YORKER (Sept. 6, 2012).

126 **"diverse and selective"**: *Grutter v. Bollinger*, 539 U.S. 306, 329 (2003).

126 **"memoir"**: Part of Justice Thomas's account in his memoir involves a conversation he had with someone who graduated from, of all places, the University of Michigan Law School: "After graduating from Yale, I met a black alumnus of the University of Michigan Law School who told me that he'd made a point of not mentioning his race on his application. I wished with all my heart that I'd done the same. By then I knew I'd made a mistake in going to Yale. I felt as though I'd been tricked, that some of the people who claimed to be helping me were in fact hurting me. This knowledge caused the anger I thought I had put behind me at Holy Cross to flare up yet again, only in a different form. I was bitter toward the white bigots whom I held responsible for the unjust treatment of blacks, but even more bitter toward those ostensibly unprejudiced whites who pretended to side with black people while using them to further their own political and social ends, turning against them when it suited their purposes." CLARENCE THOMAS, MY GRANDFATHER'S SON 110 (2007).

128 **"300 months"**: *Grutter v. Bollinger*, 539 U.S. at 346–47 (Thomas, J., dissenting) (quoting *What the Black Man Wants: An Address Delivered in Boston, Massachusetts*, on 26 January 1865, *reprinted in* THE FREDERICK DOUGLASS PAPERS 59, 68 [J. Blassingame & J. McKivigan eds., 1991]).

128 **"learn the beat"**: STEPHEN KING, ON WRITING: A MEMOIR OF THE CRAFT 129 (2002).

137 **"accumulation of paragraphs"**: SOL STEIN, STEIN ON WRITING 194 (1995).

139 **"don't require a response"**: Cecilia Watson, *How Do You Text? Unpacking the Battle between "Raindrop" and "Waterfall" Texters*, NBC NEWS (Sept. 22, 2019, 2:47 P.M.).

Part V

141 **"mesmerized by the sounds"**: ALAN LIGHTMAN, A SENSE OF THE MYSTERIOUS: SCIENCE AND THE HUMAN SPIRIT 3 (2005).

143 **"New information needs to be connected to old information"**: Eric Mazur, *Farewell, Lecture?*, Science 50 (Jan. 2009).

143 **"constant reflection"**: John Dewey, The Later Works of John Dewey, 1925–1953 177 (Jo Ann Boydston ed., 1986).

144 **"The reader is out there"**: George Saunders, Swimming in a Pond in the Rain 117 (2021).

144 **"mind is always working"**: Jerry Salz, How to Be an Artist 51 (2020).

145 **"travel after dark"**: Kathryn Schulz, *Why Animals Don't Get Lost*, New Yorker (Mar. 9, 2021).

145 **"Variation is the life of prose"**: Verlyn Klinkenborg, Several Short Sentences about Writing 55 (2012).

146 **"fully crafted paragraph"**: Leo Damrosch in Leo Damrosch, The Club: Johnson, Boswell, and the Friends Who Shaped an Age 334 (2019).

Chapter 9

149 **"fatally bossy"**: Ursula K. Le Guin, Steering the Craft: A Twenty-First Century Guide to Sailing the Sea of Story 36 (1998).

150 **"Never stop. Never settle"**: *Hennessy Very Special Launches the New Chapter in Its Never Stop Never Settle Campaign: "A New Further,"* Wines & Spirits (May 10, 2016).

150 **"Open your mind. Open your world"**: Elle Hunt, *That Heineken Ad: Brewer Tackles How to Talk to Your Political Opposite*, Guardian (Apr. 28, 2017).

150 **"elegant variation"**: Henry Watson Fowler, The King's English 177 (1908).

150 **"the allurement"**: Henry Watson Fowler, A Dictionary of Modern English Usage 180–81 (1926); *see also* Ben Yagoda, *"Arc Frays" and Other Elegant Variations*, Chron. Higher Educ. (Apr. 4, 2012); R. L. G., *"Elegant Variation," the Good and the Bad*, Economist (Apr. 4, 2012).

151 **"inelegant variation"**: Bryan A. Garner, Garner's Modern English Usage 462 (2016).

151 **"different words to refer to the same one"**: *Id.*

151 **"If different words are used"**: *Id.*

151 **"State law makes no provisions"**: Bryan A. Garner, A Dictionary of Modern Legal Usage 440 (1995).

153 **"Race matters"**: *Schuette v. Coal. to Defend Affirmative Action*, 572 U.S. 291 (2014) (Sotomayor, J., dissenting).

154 **"acts for all"**: *McCulloch v. Maryland*, 17 U.S. 316, 405 (1819).

155 **"before the other"**: David Ogilvy, Confessions of an Advertising Man (1980).

155 **"I know it when I see it"**: *Jacobellis v. Ohio*, 378 U.S. 184, 197 (1964).

156 **"undue confidence"**: Edmund Burke, Reflections on the Revolution in France 5 (1790).

156 **"boiled"**: Karl Ove Knausgaard, My Struggle: Book One 18 (Farrar, Straus and Giroux 2013) (2009).

157 **"how many"**: Gerald Stern, The Buffalo Creek Disaster: How the Survivors of One of the Worst Disasters in Coal-Mining History Brought Suit against the Coal Company—and Won 9 (1976).

157 **"You are not mistaken"**: Milton Friedman, *An Open Letter to Bill Bennett*, Wall Street J. (Sept. 7, 1989).

157 **"two"**: W. E. B. Du Bois, The Souls of Black Folk 5 (1903).

158 **"See One"**: Sanda Kotsis & Kevin Chung, *Application of See One, Do One, Teach One Concept in Surgical Training*, Plast. Reconstr. Surg. 1194 (May 2013).

158 **"Why am I compelled to write?"**: Gloria Anzaldúa, *Speaking in Tongues: A Letter to Third World Women Writers*, in The Gloria Anzaldúa Reader 30 (2009).

158 **"Here I am"**: Helen Czerski, Storm in a Teacup: The Physics of Everyday Life 250 (2017).

159 **"necessary"**: *McCulloch v. Maryland*, 17 U.S. 316 (1819).

159 **"little cakes"**: Patricia Lockwood, No One Is Talking about This 119 (2021).

161 **"young ladies"**: Walter Tevis, The Queen's Gambit 9 (1983).

161 **"even if"**: *World-Wide Volkswagen Corp. v. Woodson*, 444 U.S. 286, 294 (1980).

162 **"Where there is"**: Microsoft, *Where There's a Team, There's a Way*, YouTube (Jan. 22, 2021), https://www.youtube.com/watch?v=6bdm-14Br-s.

162 **"was broken"**: Siddhartha Mukherjee, *My Father's Body, at Rest and in Motion*, New Yorker (Jan. 1, 2018).

Chapter 10

165 **"when I became one"**: Paul Kalanithi, When Breath Becomes Air 134 (2016).

166 **"positions come alive"**: Harvard Business Review et al., HBR's 10 Must Reads on Communication 82 (2013) (reprinting Jay A. Conger, *The Necessary Art of Persuasion*, Harv. Bus. Rev. [May–Jun. 1998] at 84, 92).

166 **"compelling and tangible quality"**: *Id.*

166 **"larger than Texas"**: *Summers v. Earth Island Institute*, 555 U.S. 488 (2009) at 495.

167 **"subject to the regulations"**: *Id.*

167 **"actual or imminent"**: *Lujan v. Defenders of Wildlife*, 504 U.S. 555, 564 (1992).

167 **"tantamount to eliminating"**: *Summers v. Earth Island Institute*, 555 U.S. 488 (2009) at 496.

168 **"F-16 fighter jet"**: W. Nicholson Price II & Arti K. Rai, *Manufacturing Barriers to Biologics Competition and Innovation*, 101 Iowa L. Rev. 1023, 1024 (2016).

169 **"a seat on the Supreme Court"**: James Boyd White, Justice as Translation back cover (1994).

169 **"statistics tend to be eye-glazing"**: Chip Heath & Dan Heath, Made to Stick: Why Some Ideas Survive and Others Die 141 (2007).

169 **"more important for people to remember the relationship than the number"**: *Id.* at 143.

170 **"a 737 plane crash every day"**: Barry Nalebuff & Ian Ayres, Why Not? How to Use Everyday Ingenuity to Solve Problems Big and Small 106 (2003).

170 **"two and a half times the losses"**: Allen C. Guelzo, Gettysburg: The Last Invasion 444–45 (2013).

171 **"worst failure"**: *Id.* at 445.

171 **"more human"**: Chip Heath & Dan Heath, Made to Stick: Why Some Ideas Survive and Others Die 141 (2007).

172 **"jumped to 83 percent"**: *Id.* at 144.

172 **"no intuition"**: *Id.*

172 **"told in many places"**: *See, e.g.*, Amy J. C. Cuddy et al., *OPOWER: Increasing Energy Efficiency through Normative Influence (A)*, Harv. Bus. Rev. (Sept. 14, 2010).

173 **"conserve more themselves"**: Jonah Berger, Invisible Influence 202 (2016). *See also* P. Wesley Schultz et al., *The Constructive, Destructive, and Reconstructive Power of Social Norms*, 18 Psychol. Sci. 429 (2007).

173 **"entire year"**: *Id.* at 203.

173 **"$500 million"**: Joshua Jamerson, *Oracle to Buy Utilities-Software Maker Opower for $532 Million*, Wall Street Journal (May 2, 2016).

174 **"Imagine Kansas with just nine surgeons"**: Atul Gawande, Better: A Surgeon's Notes on Performance 188 (2007).

174 **"dinosaur is twenty-five feet high"**: Richard Feynman, *The Making of a Scientist*, Cricket (Oct. 1995)

175 **"per capita calories"**: Michael Specter, *Freedom from Fries*, New Yorker (Oct. 26, 2015).

175 **"dropping out"**: Uri Gneezy & John List, The Why Axis: Hidden Motives and the Undiscovered Economics of Everyday Life 70 (2013).

176 **"combined value"**: Evan Osnos, *Can Mark Zuckerberg Fix Facebook before It Breaks Democracy?*, New Yorker (Sept. 10, 2018).

178 **"Numbers numb our feelings"**: Tim Hindle, The Economist Guide to Management Ideas and Gurus 71 (2012).

179 **"more money than currently exists on the planet"**: Bill McKibben, *Money Is the Oxygen on Which the Fire of Global Warming Burns*, New Yorker (Sept. 17, 2019).

179 **"total cost of the program"**: Charles Kenny, Getting Better: Why Global Development Is Succeeding—and How We Can Improve the World Even More 125 (2011).

180 **"more photos are now taken"**: Erik Brynjolfsson & Andrew McAfee, The Second Machine Age: Work, Progress, and Prosperity in a Time of Brilliant Technologies 126 (2014).

180 **"nail file"**: John McPhee, Annals of the Former World 89 (1998).

181 **"size of the hole in a bagel"**: Sarah Lewis, The Rise: Creativity, the Gift of Failure, and the Search for Mastery 5 (2014).

181 **"size of Rhode Island"**: Paige Williams, *Drop Dead, Detroit!*, New Yorker (Jan. 19, 2014).

Epilogue

183 **"will my page"**: Langston Hughes, *Theme for English B*, POETRY FOUNDATION, https://www.poetryfoundation.org/poems/47880/theme-for-english-b.

184 **"bestseller"**: Sarah Lyall, *Writes, Punctuation Book and Finds It's a Best-Seller*, N.Y. TIMES (Jan. 5, 2004).

185 **"one out of three"**: Law School Admission Council, *Diversity in the US Population & the Pipeline to Legal Careers*, LSAC, https://report.lsac.org/View.aspx?Report=DiversityPopulationandPipeline.

185 **"recommended manuals"**: *See, e.g.*, Ross Guberman, *14 Great Books*, LEGAL WRITING PRO, https://www.legalwritingpro.com/articles/14-great-books/; *Legal Writing / Contract Drafting Books*, AMERICAN BAR ASSOCIATION, https://www.americanbar.org/groups/business_law/publications/writing_drafting/; legalwriting, *The Three Best Books about Writing—Are They on Your Shelf?*, LAW PROFESSOR BLOGS (Mar. 18, 2009), https://lawprofessors.typepad.com/legalwriting/2009/03/the-three-best-books-about-writing-are-they-on-your-shelf.html; *Best Sellers in Legal Education Writing*, AMAZON BEST SELLERS, https://www.amazon.com/Best-Sellers-Books-Legal-Education-Writing/zgbs/books/10929.

185 **"need to write white"**: For more on the connection between race and the teaching of writing, *see* Mya Poe, *Re-framing Race in Teaching Writing across the Curriculum*, 10 ACROSS THE DISCIPLINES 1 (Aug. 7, 2013); Chris M. Anson, *Black Holes: Writing across the Curriculum, Assessment, and the Gravitational Invisibility of Race*, in RACE AND WRITING ASSESSMENT 15 (Asao B Inoue & Mya Poe eds., 2012); Isabel Araiza et al., *Literate Practices / Language Practices: What Do We Really Know about Our Students?*, in TEACHING WRITING WITH LATINO/A STUDENTS: LESSONS LEARNED AT HISPANIC-SERVING INSTITUTIONS 87 (Cristina Kirklighter, Diana Cardenas & Susan Wolff Murphy eds., 2007).

186 **"white professors"**: For a helpful overview of the lack of diversity among clinical law faculty in particular, *see* Jon C. Dubin, *Faculty Diversity as a Clinical Legal Education Imperative*, 51 HASTINGS L. J. 445 (2000); G. S. Hans et al., *The Diversity Imperative Revisited: Racial and Gender Inclusion in Clinical Law Faculty*, 26 CLINICAL L. REV. 127 (2019).

186 **"Where's the professor?"**: *Choiceology: Season 3 Episode 5*, CHARLES SCHWAB (May 13, 2019), https://www.schwab.com/resource-center/insights/content/choiceology-season-3-episode-5.

186 **"Maybe some would say one":** *Id.*

187 **"not thought of as professorial or professional":** Larry Gordon, *Racial Minorities Feel like Outsiders at Some Colleges, USC Diversity Expert Says,* EDSOURCE (Jan. 3, 2018), https://edsource.org/2018/racial-minorities -feel-like-outsiders-at-some-colleges-usc-diversity-expert-says/591725.

191 **"dispiritingly homogenous":** *See, e.g.,* Michael J. Higdon, *Beyond the Meta-theoretical: Implicit Bias in Law Review Article Selection,* 51 WAKE FOREST L. REV. 339 (2016); Minna J. Kotkin, *Of Authorship and Audacity: An Empirical Study of Gender Disparity and Privilege in the "Top Ten" Law Reviews,* 31 WOMEN'S RTS. L. REPORTER 385 (2009); Jennifer C. Mullins & Nancy Leong, *The Persistent Gender Disparity in Student Note Publication,* 23 YALE J. L. & FEMINISM (2011); Katherine Mangan, *In Search of Diversity on Law Reviews,* CHRON. HIGHER EDUC. (Sept. 5, 2003).

PHOTO CREDITS

Introduction

Robespierre 7. "H.L.A. Hart." Licensed under CC BY-SA 4.0. https://commons.wikimedia.org/wiki/File:H.L.A.Hart.jpg.

OneArmedMan. "Sommelier F.I.S.A.R." Available in the public domain. https://commons.wikimedia.org/wiki/File:Sommelier_F.I.S.A.R..jpg.

Chapter 1

Alexander Gardner. "Abraham Lincoln O-77 Matte Collodion Print." Available in the public domain. https://commons.wikimedia.org/wiki/File:Abraham_Lincoln_O-77_matte_collodion_print.jpg.

Steve Petteway. "Ruth Bader Ginsburg, U.S. Supreme Court Justice." Available in the Public Domain. https://commons.wikimedia.org/wiki/File:Ruth_Bader_Ginsburg,_SCOTUS_photo_portrait.jpg.

Charles Sharp. "Haile Selassie Silver Plate." Licensed under CC BY-SA. https://commons.wikimedia.org/wiki/File:Haile_Selassie_silver_plate.jpg.

"Ruth Bader Ginsburg." Available in the public domain. https://commons.wikimedia.org/wiki/File:RuthBaderGinsburg.jpg.

Walter Mori. "Vladimir Nabokov." Available in the public domain of Italy. https://commons.wikimedia.org/wiki/File:Vladimir _Nabokov_1973.jpg.

Chapter 2

Time Magazine. "Gabrielle 'Coco' Chanel, 1920." Available in the public domain. https://en.wikipedia.org/wiki/File:Coco_Chanel, _1920.jpg.

Matthew W. Hutchins. "Cass Sunstein Speaking at Harvard Law School." Licensed under the CC BY 3.0. https://commons .wikimedia.org/wiki/File:Cass_Sunstein_(2008).jpg.

Haruki Murakami. "Photo Signed by Haruki Murakami." Licensed under the CC BY-SA 4.0. https://commons.wikimedia.org/wiki/ File:Photo_signed_by_Haruki_Murakami.jpg.

Rowland Scherman. "Close-up View of Vocalist Bob Dylan." Available in the public domain. https://commons.wikimedia.org/wiki/ File:Joan_Baez_Bob_Dylan_crop.jpg.

U.S. White House. "American Astronomer Sandra Faber accepts the National Medal of Science from U.S. President Barack Obama." Available in the public domain. https://commons.wikimedia.org/ wiki/File:Sandra-faber-barack-obama.png.

"W.C. Williams." Available in the public domain. https://commons .wikimedia.org/wiki/File:Wcwilliams.jpg.

Aditiv1810435. "Anton Chekhov 4 JAM." Available under CC BY-SA 4.0. https://commons.wikimedia.org/wiki/File:Anton-chekhov-4 _JAM.jpg.

Part II

Rickterto. "Flat Screen." Licensed under CC BY-SA 4.0. https:// commons.wikimedia.org/wiki/File:Flat_Screen.svg.

Chapter 3

Alexander Gardner. "Abraham Lincoln O-77 Matte Collodion Print." Available in the public domain. https://commons.wikimedia.org/wiki/File:Abraham_Lincoln_O-77_matte_collodion_print.jpg.

Chapter 4

Branch of the National Union of Journalists. "George Orwell Press Photo." Available in the public domain. https://commons.wikimedia .org/wiki/File:George_Orwell_press_photo.jpg.

Chapter 6

"Oliver Wendell Holmes, Jr. circa 1930-Edit" by Harris & Ewing is licensed under CC BY-SA.

Chapter 7

Steve Lipofsky. "Jordan by Lipofsky." Licensed under CC BY-SA 3.0. https://en.wikipedia.org/wiki/File:Jordan_by_Lipofsky _16577.jpg.

Aleksandr Osipov. "Williams Deals with a Top Spin Ball on Her Forehand." Licensed under the Creative Commons Attribution-Share Alike 2.0 Generic license. https://commons.wikimedia.org/wiki/File:Serena_Williams_Fed_Cup_%283%29.jpg.

"Ralph Ellison Photo Portrait Seated." United States Information Agency. Available in the public domain. https://commons.wikimedia .org/wiki/File:Ralph_Ellison_photo_portrait_seated.jpg.

"Denis Diderot by Louis-Michel van Loo." Available in the public domain. https://commons.wikimedia.org/wiki/File:Denis _Diderot_by_Louis-Michel_van_Loo.jpg.

Chapter 8

Library of Congress. "Sandra Day O'Connor." Available in the public domain. https://en.wikipedia.org/wiki/File:Sandra_Day_O %27Connor.jpg.

Steve Petteway. "Clarence Thomas Official SCOTUS Portrait." Available in the public domain. https://en.wikipedia.org/wiki/File: Clarence_Thomas_official_SCOTUS_portrait.jpg.

Part V

Underwood & Underwood, "John Dewey." Available in the public domain. https://commons.wikimedia.org/wiki/File:John_Dewey _cph.3a51565.jpg.

Chapter 9

Spudgfun67. "Henry Watson Fowler 1858–1933 Grammarian and Lexicographer Lived Here 1900–1903." Licensed under CC BY-SA 4.0. https://commons.wikimedia.org/ wiki/File:HENRY_WATSON_FOWLER_1858-1933 _Grammarian_and_Lexicographer_lived_here_1900-1903.jpg.

Steve Petteway. "Sonia Sotomayor in SCOTUS Robe." Available in the public domain. https://en.wikipedia.org/wiki/File:Sonia _Sotomayor_in_SCOTUS_robe.jpg.

Chapter 10

Henry Davenport Northrop. "The Battle of Gettysburg." Available in the public domain. https://commons.wikimedia.org/wiki/File: The_Battle_of_Gettysburg.jpg.

The Big T. "California Institute of Technology Professor Richard Feynman." Available in the public domain. https://commons .wikimedia.org/wiki/File:Richard_Feynman_1988.png.

CPSIA information can be obtained
at www.ICGtesting.com
Printed in the USA
JSHW011147250423
40812JS00007B/401

9 781607 857754